PASTA

MEALS IN MINUTES

THE AUSTRALIAN Women's Weekly

contents

What is it about pasta that makes it so universally loved? Composed of little more than flour and water, it hardly seems mouth-watering fare. But it features on almost everyone's list of favourite foods, perhaps because it is quick and easy to cook, accommodates any number of sauces, and is both a comforting and exciting taste sensation.

Pamela Clark

Food Director

pasta

Pasta means paste in Italian, and that's basically all it is: a mixture of coarsely ground durum wheat flour (semolina) and water worked into a dough that's extruded into a variety of shapes and used either fresh or dried. Macaroni and spaghetti are probably the most well known, but there are literally hundreds of different shapes and, to make identification even more difficult, some pasta shapes are known by different names depending on the whim of either the manufacturer or particular region. All pasta shapes are either short or long, and solid or hollow. However, after these two particular classifications, the distinctions seem to get more arbitrary, or even blurred and contradictory.

One rule of thumb in matching pasta shapes and sauces is that the longer and skinnier the pasta, the thinner and wetter the sauce (oil, cream or tomato). The sauce should cling to a pasta that is wound on the tines of a fork. Short, hollow pastas are better with chunky meat or vegetable sauces which get "trapped" in the cavities, while the delicate, more porous pastas are best served with light, brothy or creamy sauces.

At right is a list of the pasta types we are most familiar with in this country, but it is by no means exhaustive, nor does it mean that these are the only ones you can use to make the recipes in this book – experiment with different shapes until you find the one that seems "right" to you.

1 **angel hair** *(capelli d'angelo)*: small, circular nests of a very fine, delicate pasta.

2 **bow ties** *(farfalle)*: also known as butterflies; solid and dense with a frilled edge.

3 **bucatini** *(tubular spaghetti)*: long and hollow like a straw, known as perciatelli in Sicily.

4 **curly lasagne** *(pappardelle or lasagnette)*: long strips of wide, flat pasta with a scalloped edge.

5 **elbow macaroni** *(chifferi)*: short, small, curved, hollow shape.

6 **fettuccine**: ribbon pasta slightly wider than tagliolini and thinner than tagliatelle.

7 **fettuccine, spinach**: green component in the classic paglia e fieno, "straw and hay" pasta.

8 **gnocchi**: dumplings usually made of potato or semolina; can be boiled, baked or fried.

9 **linguine**: known as flat spaghetti or little tongues because of its shape.

10 **macaroni**: generic name for a wide variety of short and thick hollow pasta.

11 **orecchiette** *(little ears)*: originally a homemade specialty from Puglia, has a soft centre and chewy rim.

12 **penne**: Italian word for pen; short, straight macaroni cut on the diagonal, either smooth or grooved. Ziti are a fat penne and pennoni are a large variation.

13 **ravioli, agnolotti**: small pasta cases enclosing a savoury or sweet filling.

14 **rigatoni**: large, wide chewy macaroni, usually ridged on the surface.

15 **risoni**: regional name for a rice-shaped pastina (tiny pasta) similar to orzo, stelline and fedelini.

16 **shells, large** *(conchiglie grandi)* and **small** *(conchiglie)*: named because they look like conch shells; oblong shape pinched at the ends, available in both grooved and smooth varieties and in many sizes.

17 **spaghetti**: the shape that comes to mind when pasta is mentioned; "little strands" originally from Naples. Spaghettini is a thin version and vermicelli thinner still.

18 **spirals, large** *(fusilli)* and **small** *(fusillini)*: corkscrew or spiral-shaped short pasta; a longer variation is called fusilli lunghi; rotini are a wider, shorter, fatter corkscrew.

19 **tagliatelle**: a long ribbon pasta about 8mm in width; sometimes sold in nests resembling egg noodles.

20 **tortellini**: a pasta ripieni (stuffed pasta) similar to ravioli but made in the shape of a ring or small cap.

pasta perfect

No matter how great your sauce or accompaniments might be, if the pasta isn't of good quality or if it hasn't been cooked properly, the finished dish will not be a success.

1 Bring large saucepan of water to a rolling boil, allowing approximately 3 litres of water and 1 teaspoon of salt for every 250g pasta. Add pasta to pan and allow water to return to a boil.

2 As soon as pasta becomes pliable enough to bend, stir with a pasta fork to separate strands or pieces. Continue stirring occasionally during cooking. For dried pasta, use the manufacturer's recommended cooking time as a guide, but test 1 to 2 minutes short of the suggested time. The degree of tenderness is very much a matter of personal taste, though most pasta lovers prefer theirs al dente, slightly firm to the bite.

3 When cooked, drain the pasta into a large colander over the sink, shaking or swirling colander to make sure all water drains away. Divide pasta among bowls or place in large serving bowl, add sauce and serve immediately.

To reheat pasta, you can use either of these methods.

Method 1 With pasta still in colander, place over a large saucepan; pour boiling water over pasta, allowing water to drain into pan. Separate pasta pieces with a pasta fork, then lift from colander to drain.

Method 2 After initially draining pasta, allow to cool in a colander until you can handle it. Using your hands, work 2 tablespoons of olive oil through the slightly cooled pasta. Later, when required, reheat pasta by plunging it from the colander into a large saucepan of boiling water, then draining it immediately in the same colander.

A well-stocked pantry and refrigerator enable you to prepare a meal in minutes.

You'll always be able to whip up easy pasta dishes in a hurry if you keep ingredients such as these on hand in the fridge or cupboard.

- dried pasta of various shapes and sizes

- cryovac packages of fresh lasagne sheets, ravioli, gnocchi, etc

- extra-virgin, virgin and light olive oil

- red wine, white wine and balsamic vinegars

- parmesan, pepato and romano cheese

- bacon, prosciutto and pancetta

- eggs

- capers, caperberries

- black and green olives

- anchovies

- fresh lemons

- sun-dried and semi-dried tomatoes

- canned sardines, canned tuna, canned salmon

- canned tomatoes, canned tomato puree, canned tomato paste

- good-quality bottled tomato pasta sauce (sugo)

- canned or bottled artichoke hearts

- pine nuts, almonds

- fresh herbs such as oregano, basil, coriander, thyme, etc

- garlic, chillies and onions

- fresh salad leaves

salads

The idea of starring pasta in a salad may have evolved from the Italian habit of serving leftover pasta dishes cold, but these delicious and eye-catching recipes owe far more to mouth-watering innovation than to any tradition.

roasted capsicum, goat cheese and walnut salad

PREPARATION TIME 10 MINUTES • COOKING TIME 20 MINUTES

375g large spirals
2 medium red capsicums (400g)
2 medium yellow capsicums (400g)
150g goat cheese, crumbled
1/3 cup (35g) walnuts, toasted, chopped coarsely
1/2 cup loosely packed fresh basil leaves
1/4 cup (60ml) red wine vinegar
1/3 cup (80ml) olive oil
1 clove garlic, crushed
2 teaspoons seeded mustard

1 Cook pasta in large saucepan of boiling water, uncovered, until just tender; drain. Rinse under cold water; drain.

2 Meanwhile, quarter capsicums, remove and discard seeds and membranes. Roast under grill or in very hot oven, skin-side up, until skin blisters and blackens. Cover capsicum pieces with plastic or paper for 5 minutes, peel away skin; slice capsicum thickly.

3 Place pasta and capsicum in large bowl with cheese, walnuts, basil and combined remaining ingredients; toss gently to combine.

SERVES 4

per serving 31.5g fat; 2703kJ

tip Fetta or any soft, crumbly cheese can be used instead of the goat cheese, and toasted pecan halves make a nice change from walnuts.

greek penne salad

PREPARATION TIME 15 MINUTES • COOKING TIME 15 MINUTES

250g penne
250g fetta cheese
4 medium tomatoes (760g),
    seeded, sliced thinly
1 lebanese cucumber (130g),
    seeded, sliced thinly
1 small red onion (100g),
    sliced thinly
3/4 cup (120g) kalamata
    olives, seeded
3/4 cup (120g) large green
    olives, seeded
1/3 cup (80ml) olive oil
1/3 cup (80ml) white vinegar
1 teaspoon sugar
2 tablespoons finely chopped
    fresh flat-leaf parsley

1 Cook pasta in large saucepan of boiling water, uncovered, until just tender; drain. Rinse under cold water; drain.

2 Meanwhile, cut fetta into baton-shape pieces approximately the same size as the pasta.

3 Place pasta and fetta in large bowl with tomato, cucumber, onion, olives and combined remaining ingredients; toss gently to combine.

SERVES 4

per serving 34.1g fat; 2694kJ

tip This salad is a perfect match for lemon-marinated lamb skewers.

mediterranean salad

PREPARATION TIME 10 MINUTES • COOKING TIME 15 MINUTES

375g elbow macaroni
350g artichoke hearts in oil
400g semi-dried tomatoes
1/4 cup loosely packed
    fresh oregano
400g bocconcini cheese,
    chopped coarsely
1/4 cup (60ml) sherry vinegar
2 cloves garlic, crushed

1 Cook pasta in large saucepan of boiling water, uncovered, until just tender; drain. Rinse under cold water; drain.

2 Meanwhile, drain artichokes over small bowl; reserve 2 tablespoons of the oil. Discard any remaining oil; quarter artichokes.

3 Place pasta and artichoke in large bowl with tomatoes, oregano, cheese and combined vinegar, garlic and reserved oil; toss gently to combine.

SERVES 4

per serving 34.4g fat; 3322kJ

tip This salad is perfect to pack in a leak-proof container and take on a picnic.

ravioli salad

PREPARATION TIME 15 MINUTES • COOKING TIME 15 MINUTES

You need approximately 500g of fresh broccoli for this recipe, and you can use any variety of ravioli you like so long as the filling does not include any meat.

375g spinach and ricotta ravioli
4 (280g) bacon rashers, chopped coarsely
250g (2 cups) broccoli florets
250g cherry tomatoes, halved
2 tablespoons finely shredded fresh basil leaves
1/2 cup (125ml) olive oil
1/4 cup (60ml) white wine vinegar
2 tablespoons sun-dried tomato pesto

1 Cook pasta in large saucepan of boiling water, uncovered, until just tender; drain. Rinse under cold water; drain.

2 Meanwhile, cook bacon in small frying pan, stirring, until browned and crisp; drain on absorbent paper.

3 Boil, steam or microwave broccoli until just tender, drain. Rinse under cold water; drain.

4 Place ravioli, bacon and broccoli in large bowl with tomato, basil and combined remaining ingredients; toss gently to combine.

SERVES 4

per serving 37.9g fat; 2205kJ

serving suggestion This salad can serve as the main course for a light lunch or late supper, accompanied by a simple green salad and a loaf of fresh bread.

tip You can use any kind of prepared pesto you prefer in this salad's dressing: roasted vegetable is a good alternative.

smoked salmon and dill salad

PREPARATION TIME 10 MINUTES • COOKING TIME 15 MINUTES

250g bucatini
2 small bulbs fennel (600g),
trimmed, sliced thinly
1 medium red onion (170g),
sliced thinly
200g smoked salmon,
sliced thickly
1/4 cup drained capers,
chopped coarsely
1/2 cup loosely packed
fresh dill tips
1/2 cup (125ml) crème fraîche
2 teaspoons finely grated
lemon rind
1/4 cup (60ml) lemon juice

1 Cook pasta in large saucepan of boiling water, uncovered, until just tender; drain. Rinse under cold water; drain.

2 Place pasta in large bowl with fennel, onion, salmon, capers, dill and combined remaining ingredients; toss gently to combine.

SERVES 4

per serving 15.2g fat; 1784kJ

tips The salad can be prepared several hours ahead and kept, covered, in the refrigerator. Pour over combined crème fraîche, rind and juice just before serving.

You can substitute the crème fraîche with sour cream, light sour cream or thick cream if you prefer.

sweet chilli prawn salad

PREPARATION TIME 10 MINUTES • COOKING TIME 10 MINUTES

250g rigatoni
24 large cooked shelled
  prawns (approximately 1kg),
  tails intact
2 green onions, chopped finely
1 tablespoon coarsely chopped
  fresh watercress
1 tablespoon coarsely chopped
  fresh coriander leaves
1 lebanese cucumber (130g),
  chopped coarsely
¹/₂ cup (125ml) sweet chilli sauce
1 teaspoon sesame oil
1 tablespoon lime juice

1 Cook pasta in large saucepan of boiling water, uncovered, until tender; drain. Rinse under cold water; drain.

2 Place pasta in large bowl with prawns, onion, watercress, coriander, cucumber and combined remaining ingredients; toss gently to combine.

SERVES 4

per serving 3.5g fat; 1552kJ

tip We used Thai sweet chilli sauce; if you use a less sweet, more concentrated chilli sauce, we suggest you use far less, tasting as you go.

bow ties with asparagus and grilled haloumi

PREPARATION TIME 10 MINUTES • COOKING TIME 20 MINUTES

250g bow ties
750g asparagus, trimmed, chopped coarsely
250g haloumi cheese, sliced thinly
1 medium avocado (250g), sliced thinly
2 tablespoons coarsely chopped fresh chives
1 tablespoon finely grated lemon rind
1/4 cup (60ml) lemon juice
1/3 cup (80ml) olive oil
1 teaspoon sugar

1 Cook pasta in large saucepan of boiling water, uncovered, until just tender; drain. Rinse under cold water; drain.

2 Meanwhile, boil, steam or microwave asparagus until just tender; drain.

3 Cook cheese, in batches, in medium frying pan until browned lightly; drain on absorbent paper.

4 Place pasta, asparagus and cheese in large bowl with avocado, chives and combined remaining ingredients; toss gently to combine.

SERVES 4

per serving 47.7g fat; 2974kJ

tip If you can spare the extra time, after breaking off the woody ends from asparagus spears, halve the spears and cook them on a lightly oiled grill plate or under a grill until just tender and browned lightly.

lamb and pasta with walnut coriander pesto

PREPARATION TIME 10 MINUTES • COOKING TIME 15 MINUTES

You need approximately two bunches of fresh coriander for this recipe, including the roots and stems as well as the leaves.

375g bow ties
4 (320g) lamb fillets
1¹/₂ cups firmly packed, coarsely
   chopped fresh coriander
¹/₂ cup (50g) walnuts, toasted
¹/₂ cup (40g) coarsely grated
   parmesan cheese
2 cloves garlic, quartered
¹/₂ cup (125ml) light olive oil
1 tablespoon drained preserved
   lemons, chopped finely
¹/₂ cup (140g) yogurt
2 teaspoons light olive oil, extra
2 teaspoons lemon juice

1 Cook pasta in large saucepan of boiling water, uncovered, until just tender; drain. Rinse under cold water; drain.

2 Meanwhile, cook lamb in large non-stick frying pan until browned all over and cooked as desired. Stand 5 minutes; cut into thin slices.

3 Reserve 2 tablespoons of coriander leaves. Blend or process nuts, remaining coriander, cheese, garlic and oil until mixture forms a smooth paste. Combine pesto with pasta in large bowl.

4 Divide pasta mixture among serving plates, top with lamb and lemon; drizzle salad with combined yogurt, oil and juice, top with reserved coriander leaves.

SERVES 4

per serving 47.7g fat; 3477kJ

russian penne salad

PREPARATION TIME 15 MINUTES • COOKING TIME 10 MINUTES

This new take on the classic Russian original is great served with pork loin chops.

375g penne
2 cups (250g) frozen peas
450g can whole baby beets,
   drained, chopped coarsely
6 green onions, chopped finely
2 cloves garlic, crushed
2 large dill pickles,
   chopped finely
1/4 cup loosely packed, coarsely
   chopped fresh flat-leaf parsley
1 cup (240g) sour cream
1 cup (250ml) buttermilk

1 Cook pasta in large saucepan of boiling water, uncovered, until just tender; drain. Rinse under cold water; drain.

2 Meanwhile, boil, steam or microwave peas until just tender; drain.

3 Place pasta and peas in large bowl with beet, onion, garlic, pickle, parsley and combined cream and buttermilk; toss gently to combine.

SERVES 4

per serving 26.6g fat; 2753kJ

pasta caesar salad

PREPARATION TIME 15 MINUTES • COOKING TIME 15 MINUTES

200g large shells
2 (140g) bacon rashers, chopped finely
1 medium cos lettuce, torn
2 hard-boiled eggs, chopped coarsely
2 small avocados (400g), chopped coarsely
1/2 cup (40g) shaved parmesan cheese

CAESAR DRESSING
1 egg
2 cloves garlic, quartered
2 tablespoons lemon juice
1 teaspoon dijon mustard
8 anchovy fillets, drained
3/4 cup (180ml) olive oil

1 Cook pasta in large saucepan of boiling water, uncovered, until just tender; drain. Rinse under cold water; drain.

2 Meanwhile, cook bacon in small frying pan, stirring, until browned and crisp; drain on absorbent paper.

3 Place pasta and bacon in large bowl with lettuce, hard-boiled egg and avocado; pour over half of the caesar dressing, toss gently to combine.

4 Divide salad among serving plates; drizzle with remaining dressing, sprinkle with cheese.

caesar dressing Blend or process egg, garlic, juice, mustard and anchovies until smooth; with motor operating, gradually add oil, processing until dressing thickens.

SERVES 4

per serving 68.1g fat; 3611kJ
tip Caesar dressing can be prepared a day ahead.

spinach and prosciutto salad

PREPARATION TIME 10 MINUTES • COOKING TIME 10 MINUTES

375g large spirals
12 thin slices prosciutto (240g)
150g baby spinach leaves
2 tablespoons seeded mustard
2 cloves garlic, crushed
1/2 cup (125ml) olive oil
1/4 cup (60ml) lemon juice

1 Cook pasta in large saucepan of boiling water, uncovered, until tender; drain. Rinse under cold water; drain.

2 Meanwhile, cook prosciutto, in batches, in large heated frying pan until browned and crisp; drain on absorbent paper, chop coarsely.

3 Place pasta and prosciutto in large bowl with spinach and combined remaining ingredients; toss gently to combine.

SERVES 4

per serving 33.3g fat; 2738kJ

tip Finely slice or chop two hard-boiled eggs, if you wish, and toss them through this salad just before serving.

chicken, hazelnut and rocket salad

PREPARATION TIME 5 MINUTES • COOKING TIME 15 MINUTES

250g linguine
340g chicken breast fillets
1/2 cup (75g) hazelnuts, toasted,
** chopped coarsely**
100g curly endive
150g baby rocket leaves
1/3 cup (80ml) lime juice
1/3 cup (80ml) olive oil
2 cloves garlic, crushed
2 teaspoons dijon mustard

1 Cook pasta in large saucepan of boiling water, uncovered, until just tender; drain. Rinse pasta under cold water; drain.

2 Meanwhile, cook chicken on heated oiled grill plate (or grill or barbecue) until browned all over and cooked through. Stand 5 minutes; cut into thin slices.

3 Combine pasta and chicken in large bowl with hazelnuts, endive, rocket and combined remaining ingredients; toss gently to combine.

SERVES 4

per serving 35.6g fat; 2593kJ

seafood salad

PREPARATION TIME 5 MINUTES • COOKING TIME 20 MINUTES

1 teaspoon olive oil
1 small brown onion (80g), sliced thinly
1 clove garlic, crushed
500g seafood marinara mix
375g large shells
1 tablespoon dry white wine
1/2 cup (150g) mayonnaise
1 teaspoon lemon juice
2 teaspoons worcestershire sauce
1/3 cup (80ml) tomato sauce
1/4 teaspoon Tabasco sauce
1 tablespoon coarsely chopped fresh flat-leaf parsley
100g baby rocket leaves

1 Heat oil in large frying pan; cook onion and garlic, stirring, until onion softens. Add marinara mix; cook, stirring, about 5 minutes or until seafood is cooked through. Place marinara mixture in large bowl, cover; refrigerate until cold.

2 Meanwhile, cook pasta in large saucepan of boiling water, uncovered, until just tender; drain. Rinse under cold water; drain.

3 Place pasta and combined wine, mayonnaise, juice, sauces and parsley in bowl with marinara mixture; toss gently to combine. Serve seafood salad on rocket leaves.

SERVES 4

per serving 15.2g fat; 2650kJ

pasta with the lot

PREPARATION TIME 10 MINUTES • COOKING TIME 15 MINUTES

*Swiss brown mushrooms are also called roman or cremini mushrooms; use ordinary fresh
button mushrooms if you can't easily find them.*

250g curly lasagne
150g spanish salami,
  sliced thickly
200g swiss brown mushrooms,
  sliced thickly
1 medium green capsicum (200g),
  sliced thinly
2 medium tomatoes (380g),
  seeded, sliced thinly
4 anchovies, drained,
  chopped coarsely
100g kalamata olives, seeded
1/2 cup (125ml) vegetable juice
1/4 cup (60ml) red wine vinegar
1/4 cup (60ml) olive oil
2 cloves garlic, crushed

1 Cook pasta in large saucepan of boiling water, uncovered, until
   just tender; drain. Rinse under cold water; drain.

2 Place pasta in large bowl with salami, mushrooms, capsicum,
   tomato, anchovy, olives and combined remaining ingredients;
   toss gently to combine.

SERVES 4

per serving 29.3g fat; 2296kJ

tip We used a hot and spicy spanish salami in this recipe but you
could use milder cabanossi or peperoni, if you prefer. You can also use
tomato juice in the dressing, if you wish, instead of the vegetable juice.

fresh tomato and caper salsa with penne

PREPARATION TIME 15 MINUTES • COOKING TIME 10 MINUTES

375g penne
6 medium tomatoes (1.1kg),
  seeded, chopped finely
¹/₃ cup (80g) drained capers,
  chopped coarsely
1 medium red onion (170g),
  chopped finely
12 basil leaves, torn
12 purple basil leaves, torn
¹/₂ cup (80g) toasted pine nuts

BALSAMIC VINAIGRETTE
2 cloves garlic, crushed
¹/₃ cup (80ml) balsamic vinegar
²/₃ cup (160ml) olive oil

1 Cook pasta in large saucepan of boiling water, uncovered, until tender; drain. Rinse until cold water; drain.

2 Place pasta in large bowl with remaining ingredients; drizzle with balsamic vinaigrette, toss gently to combine.

balsamic vinaigrette Combine garlic, vinegar and oil in screw-top jar; shake well.

SERVES 4

per serving 51.7g fat; 2297kJ

macaroni tuna salad

PREPARATION TIME 15 MINUTES • COOKING TIME 15 MINUTES

250g small macaroni
200g green beans, halved
200g yellow string beans, halved
415g can tuna in oil, drained, flaked
1 small red onion (80g), sliced thinly
1/4 cup loosely packed, finely chopped fresh flat-leaf parsley
1/2 cup (125ml) olive oil
1/4 cup (60ml) lemon juice
2 cloves garlic, crushed
2 teaspoons curry powder

1 Cook pasta in large saucepan of boiling water, uncovered, until just tender; drain. Rinse under cold water; drain.

2 Meanwhile, boil, steam or microwave beans until just tender; drain. Rinse under cold water; drain.

3 Place pasta and beans in large bowl with tuna, onion, parsley and combined remaining ingredients; toss gently to combine.

SERVES 4

per serving 49.1g fat; 3091kJ

tip Yellow string beans are sometimes called butter beans; you can substitute them with chopped snake beans if desired.

cheese and eggs

These two mainstays of the kitchen lend themselves particularly well to being combined with various pastas, herbs and vegetables, and, in fact, some of the smartest and quickest Italian classics fall into this category.

spaghetti with herbed ricotta

PREPARATION TIME 10 MINUTES • COOKING TIME 15 MINUTES

450g fresh ricotta
3 egg yolks
³/₄ cup (180ml) milk
¹/₃ cup firmly packed, coarsely chopped fresh flat-leaf parsley
¹/₄ cup firmly packed, coarsely chopped fresh basil leaves
3 green onions, chopped finely
2 cloves garlic, crushed
¹/₄ cup (20g) finely grated pepato cheese
500g spaghetti

1 Cook pasta in large saucepan of boiling water, uncovered, until just tender; drain.

2 Whisk ricotta, egg yolks and milk in large bowl until smooth; stir in herbs, onion, garlic and cheese.

3 Add pasta to ricotta mixture; toss gently to combine.

SERVES 4

per serving 21.7g fat; 2863kJ·

tip If you prefer, substitute the pepato with another hard cheese, such as romano or an aged provolone, and feel free to use other herbs, such as chives or oregano, instead of the basil.

macaroni cheese

PREPARATION TIME 5 MINUTES • COOKING TIME 20 MINUTES

250g elbow macaroni
60g butter
1/3 cup (50g) plain flour
3 cups (750ml) milk
2 cups (250g) coarsely grated
  pizza cheese

1 Cook pasta in large saucepan of boiling water, uncovered, until just tender; drain. While pasta is cooking, melt butter in medium saucepan, add flour; cook, stirring, about 2 minutes or until mixture thickens and bubbles. Gradually stir in milk; cook, stirring, until sauce boils and thickens.

2 Stir pasta and half of the cheese into sauce; pour mixture into shallow 2-litre (8-cup) baking dish. Sprinkle with remaining cheese; place under hot grill until cheese melts and is browned lightly.

SERVES 4

per serving 34.2g fat; 2846kJ.

tip This quick version doesn't have to go into the oven, like the traditional macaroni cheese recipe, so it's great when you want dinner on the table fast.

fettuccine carbonara

PREPARATION TIME 10 MINUTES • COOKING TIME 10 MINUTES

*Named for a pasta sauce made by Italian charcoal-makers, and so easy to prepare it could be whipped up
in a single pot hung over the fire out in the forest, carbonara has come to represent the classic easy creamy
pasta sauce. You can use pancetta or prosciutto instead of the bacon if you prefer.*

**4 (280g) bacon rashers,
chopped coarsely**
375g fettuccine
3 egg yolks, beaten lightly
1 cup (250ml) cream
**1/2 cup (30g) finely grated
parmesan cheese**
**2 tablespoons coarsely chopped
fresh chives**

1 Cook bacon in heated small frying pan, stirring, until crisp; drain.

2 Just before serving, cook pasta in large saucepan of boiling water,
uncovered, until just tender; drain.

3 Combine pasta in large bowl with egg yolks, cream and cheese;
sprinkle with chives.

SERVES 4

per serving 34.2g fat; 2762kJ

tip Try using grated romano or pepato instead of parmesan.

gnocchi al quattro formaggi

PREPARATION TIME 10 MINUTES
COOKING TIME 10 MINUTES

Pasta with four cheeses is one of the most delectable (and among the richest!) of all the Italian classic sauces. Here, we team it with gnocchi, but it also marries well with fettuccine or tagliatelle.

1/4 cup (60ml) dry white wine
1 cup (250g) mascarpone cheese
1 cup (120g) coarsely grated fontina cheese
1/2 cup (40g) coarsely grated parmesan cheese
1/4 cup (60ml) milk
625g gnocchi
75g gorgonzola cheese, crumbled

1 Add wine to large saucepan; boil, uncovered, until wine reduces by half. Reduce heat, add mascarpone; stir until mixture is smooth. Add fontina, parmesan and milk; cook, stirring, until cheeses melt and sauce is smooth in consistency.

2 Meanwhile, cook gnocchi in large saucepan of boiling water, uncovered, until gnocchi rise to the surface and are just tender; drain.

3 Add gnocchi and gorgonzola to sauce; toss gently to combine.

SERVES 4

per serving 52.3g fat; 3068kJ

tip If this pasta dish, with its sauce of four cheeses, is served as a first course, try not to follow it with a main course that's equally rich. Grilled plain chops or poached fish fillets are perfect possibilities.

bucatini with baked ricotta

PREPARATION TIME 5 MINUTES • COOKING TIME 15 MINUTES

**2 x 270g jars marinated
  eggplant in oil**
2 cloves garlic, crushed
375g bucatini
2 x 415g cans tomatoes
1/2 teaspoon cracked black pepper
**300g baked ricotta,
  chopped coarsely**

1 Cook undrained eggplant and garlic in large saucepan, stirring, until fragrant. Meanwhile, cook pasta in large saucepan of boiling water, uncovered, until just tender; drain.

2 Stir pasta, undrained crushed tomatoes and pepper into eggplant mixture; toss over medium heat until combined, then gently stir in ricotta.

SERVES 4

per serving 32.4g fat; 3352kJ

tip You can use any kind of marinated vegetables (mushrooms, capsicum or mixed antipasti) in this recipe instead of the eggplant.

fettuccine alfredo

PREPARATION TIME 10 MINUTES • COOKING TIME 20 MINUTES

A Roman restaurateur first developed this eponymous dish in 1914, tossing it together at the table before his customers' eyes with his fabled gold fork and spoon. We've made our updated version on the stove-top and, to cut back on the fat content, omitted the copious amount of butter he used.

375g fettuccine
2 teaspoons olive oil
4 green onions, sliced thinly
1 clove garlic, crushed
2 tablespoons dry white wine
300ml cream
1 teaspoon dijon mustard
1/4 cup loosely packed, finely chopped fresh flat-leaf parsley
1 cup (80g) finely grated parmesan cheese

1 Cook pasta in large saucepan of boiling water, uncovered, until just tender; drain.

2 While pasta is cooking, heat oil in medium saucepan; cook onion and garlic, stirring, until onion softens. Add wine and cream; bring to a boil. Reduce heat; simmer, stirring, about 2 minutes or until sauce is smooth. Stir in mustard.

3 Add pasta, parsley and cheese to sauce; toss gently to combine.

SERVES 4

per serving 43g fat; 3148kJ

angel hair frittata

PREPARATION TIME 10 MINUTES • COOKING TIME 20 MINUTES

100g angel hair pasta
1 tablespoon vegetable oil
1 small leek (200g), chopped coarsely
2 cloves garlic, crushed
1/4 cup (20g) finely grated parmesan cheese
200g fetta cheese, crumbled
60g spinach leaves, chopped coarsely
1/2 cup (120g) sour cream
1/4 teaspoon ground nutmeg
6 eggs, beaten lightly

1 Cook pasta in large saucepan of boiling water, uncovered, until just tender; drain.

2 While pasta is cooking, heat oil in 20cm frying pan; cook leek and garlic, stirring, until leek softens.

3 Combine pasta and leek mixture in large bowl with cheeses, spinach, sour cream, nutmeg and egg. Pour mixture into same frying pan, cover; cook over low heat for 10 minutes.

4 Remove cover; place under heated grill for about 5 minutes or until frittata sets and top browns lightly. Stand in pan 5 minutes before serving.

SERVES 4

per serving 38.4g fat; 2202kJ

tip Angel hair pasta, the finest of pastas, produces the best results in this frittata because it lends a smooth-textured consistency.

rigatoni with brie, walnut and mushroom sauce

PREPARATION TIME 5 MINUTES • COOKING TIME 20 MINUTES

1 tablespoon olive oil
1 clove garlic, crushed
200g button mushrooms, halved
1/2 cup (125ml) dry white wine
2 tablespoons seeded mustard
600ml light cream
375g rigatoni
200g brie cheese, chopped coarsely
1 cup (100g) walnuts, toasted, chopped coarsely
1/4 cup coarsely chopped fresh chives

1 Heat oil in large frying pan; cook garlic and mushrooms, stirring, until mushrooms are just tender. Add wine; boil, uncovered, until wine reduces by half.

2 Add mustard and cream to mushroom mixture; cook, stirring, until sauce thickens slightly.

3 Meanwhile, cook pasta in large saucepan of boiling water, uncovered, until just tender; drain.

4 Place pasta, cheese, walnuts, chives and sauce in large bowl; toss gently to combine.

SERVES 4

per serving 77.7g fat; 4686kJ

tomato and bacon macaroni cheese

PREPARATION TIME 10 MINUTES • COOKING TIME 25 MINUTES

185g small shell pasta
4 (280g) bacon rashers,
   chopped coarsely
80g butter
1 medium brown onion (150g),
   chopped finely
1 medium green capsicum (200g),
   chopped finely
1 teaspoon mustard powder
1/2 teaspoon sweet paprika
1/4 cup (35g) plain flour
1 cup (250ml) milk
420g can tomato soup
11/2 cups (190g) coarsely grated
   cheddar cheese
1 teaspoon worcestershire sauce

1 Cook pasta in large saucepan of boiling water, uncovered, until just tender; drain.

2 While pasta is cooking, cook bacon in heated dry large saucepan, stirring, until brown all over; drain on absorbent paper.

3 Melt butter in same cleaned saucepan; cook onion and capsicum, stirring, until vegetables soften. Add bacon, mustard and paprika; cook, stirring, 2 minutes. Add flour; cook, stirring, until mixture bubbles and thickens. Gradually stir in milk and soup; cook, stirring, until soup mixture boils and thickens.

4 Stir pasta, two-thirds of the cheese, and sauce into soup mixture; pour mixture into shallow 1.5-litre (6-cup) rectangular ovenproof dish. Sprinkle with remaining cheese; place under hot grill until cheese melts and top is browned lightly.

SERVES 4

per serving 36.9g fat; 2749kJ

tip You can substitute pizza cheese and chopped salami for the cheddar and bacon, if you prefer.

roasted kumara and parmesan with curly lasagne

PREPARATION TIME 10 MINUTES • COOKING TIME 25 MINUTES

In this recipe we've used broken curly lasagne, sometimes called pappardelle or lasagnette, for the casual look we wanted with the kumara.

1 large kumara (500g)
2 tablespoons olive oil
250g curly lasagne
1 cup (80g) shaved
   parmesan cheese
250g rocket leaves, torn
1/4 cup (60ml) balsamic vinegar
1/4 cup (60ml) olive oil, extra
1 clove garlic, crushed

1 Preheat oven to very hot. Halve kumara lengthways; slice halves into 5mm pieces. Combine kumara with oil in large baking dish; roast, uncovered, in very hot oven about 25 minutes or until tender.

2 Meanwhile, break pasta roughly lengthways, cook in large saucepan of boiling water, uncovered, until just tender; drain.

3 Place pasta, kumara, cheese, rocket and combined remaining ingredients in large bowl; toss gently to combine.

SERVES 4

per serving 30.5g fat; 2500kJ

penne, parmesan and asparagus hollandaise

PREPARATION TIME 15 MINUTES • COOKING TIME 15 MINUTES

1/4 cup (60ml) white vinegar
1 tablespoon coarsely chopped fresh tarragon leaves
8 whole black peppercorns
4 egg yolks
250g cold unsalted butter, chopped
1 tablespoon lemon juice
375g penne
1kg asparagus, trimmed, chopped coarsely
1/3 cup (25g) grated parmesan cheese

1 Combine vinegar, tarragon and peppercorns in small saucepan; bring to a boil. Reduce heat; simmer, uncovered, until mixture reduces to about 1 tablespoon. Strain vinegar reduction into large heatproof bowl, discard tarragon and peppercorns.

2 Place bowl containing vinegar reduction over large saucepan of simmering water; whisk in egg yolks until mixture is light and fluffy. Gradually add butter, whisking continuously between additions, until hollandaise sauce thickens; stir in juice.

3 Cook pasta in large saucepan of boiling water, uncovered, until just tender; drain. While pasta is cooking, boil, steam or microwave asparagus until just tender; drain.

4 Place pasta, asparagus, cheese and hollandaise sauce in large bowl; toss gently to combine.

SERVES 4

per serving 56.5g fat; 3580kJ

tip Be careful not to have heat too high when whisking egg yolks with the vinegar reduction, or you'll end up with scrambled eggs rather than a smooth hollandaise.

cheese and spinach tortellini with gorgonzola sauce

PREPARATION TIME 5 MINUTES • COOKING TIME 15 MINUTES

Gorgonzola is the traditional northern Italian creamy blue cheese used in pasta sauces, dips and salads. The double-cream Bavarian blue or Blue Castello can be substituted but will lack that particular tempered piquancy of a ripe gorgonzola.

30g butter
2 tablespoons plain flour
1 cup (250ml) milk
³/₄ cup (180ml) cream
100g gorgonzola cheese, chopped coarsely
750g cheese and spinach tortellini
¹/₄ cup loosely packed fresh flat-leaf parsley

1 Melt butter in medium saucepan, add flour; cook, stirring, about 2 minutes or until mixture thickens and bubbles.

2 Gradually stir in milk and cream; bring to a boil. Reduce heat; simmer, uncovered, until sauce boils and thickens. Remove from heat; stir in cheese.

3 Meanwhile, cook pasta in large saucepan of boiling water, uncovered, until just tender; drain.

4 Combine pasta with sauce, sprinkle with parsley.

SERVES 4

per serving 43.8g fat; 3017kJ

tips You can substitute the tortellini with ravioli or even gnocchi, if you prefer.

It's best to choose a ricotta-and-spinach-filled tortellini (or the even-simpler ricotta-filled version) when making this sauce, as it doesn't marry overly well with meat-filled pastas.

parmesan & more

While most of the cheeses that usually accompany pasta originated in Italy, versions are now produced all over the world. And, in our collection of recipes, we've borrowed a few other national favourites — such as fetta from Greece and brie from France — to temper the mix.

Asiago Originally made from sheep milk, this Italian cheese is now most often made from cow milk. There are three types of asiago: the first, pressato, is a lightly pressed cheese, semi-ripe, with a delicate, sweet flavour; the second, asiago d'allevo, is a matured hard cheese made with skim milk and aged up to two years; the last, asiago grasso di monte, is a soft, full-cream cheese made from the milk of cows that have grazed from pastures situated a minimum 1000m above sea level.

Brie Often referred to as the "queen of cheeses", brie was first recorded during the 8th century when Charles the Great, later Holy Roman Emperor Charlemagne, was visiting the Ile de France region and ordered two batches to be sent to him annually. Smooth and voluptuous, brie has a bloomy white rind and a creamy centre which becomes runnier as it ripens.

Cheddar The most widely eaten cheese in the world, cheddar is a semi-hard cow milk cheese originally made in England. It ranges in colour from almost white to pale orange, and has a crumbly texture when properly matured. It's aged for between nine months and two years; the flavour becomes sharper with time.
Fetta A white cheese with milky, fresh acidity, fetta is one of the cornerstones of the Greek, Turkish and Bulgarian kitchens. Its provenance is ancient, with Homer giving a detailed description of how to make it in the Odyssey. Today, it is most commonly made from cow milk, though sheep and goat milk varieties are available. Fetta

pecorino

fontina

mozzarella

parmesan

pepato

is sometimes described as a pickled cheese because it is matured in brine for at least a month, which imparts a strong salty flavour. Fetta is solid, but crumbles readily.

Fontina Originating from the Valle d'Aosta region of the Italian Alps near the Swiss and French borders, fontina is a smooth, firm cheese with a sweet, nutty flavour and pale yellow colour. Made from cow milk, it's usually matured for about three months in caves, tunnels and even abandoned mines, which may explain its slightly earthy overtone.

Gorgonzola Originally from the Lombardy region of Italy, this creamy, cow milk blue cheese is pierced with needles of *penicillium glaucum* at about four weeks to encourage the mould to spread. It takes about three to six months to mature fully, by which time the colour ranges from white to straw-yellow with bluish-green marbling from the mould. **Dolcelatte**, or sweet milk cheese, is produced by a similar method, except that it's made from the curd of only one milking and has a milder flavour. **Blue Castello**, a cow milk cheese developed in Denmark in the 1960s, could be substituted for gorgonzola or dolcelatte.

Mascarpone Another product from the Lombardy region of southern Italy, mascarpone is a cultured, very soft cream cheese made in much the same way as yogurt. It is whitish to creamy-yellow in colour, with a soft, creamy texture, a fat content of 75% and a slightly tangy taste.

Mozzarella This soft, spun-curd cheese originated in southern Italy where it is traditionally made from water buffalo milk. Cow milk versions of this product (commonly thought of as the cheese used on pizza) are now available. It has a low melting point and wonderfully elastic texture when heated, and is used to add texture rather than flavour.

Bocconcini, from the Italian word boccone, meaning mouthful, is the term used for walnut- to golf-ball-sized fresh baby mozzarella.

Parmesan The Italian parmigiano is a hard, grainy cow milk cheese which originated in the Parma region of Italy. The curd is salted in brine for a month before being aged for up to two years in humid conditions. Parmesan is mainly grated as a topping for pasta, soups and other savoury dishes, but it is also delicious eaten with fruit.

Parmigiano reggiano can only be made in the Emilia-Romagna region from the milk of cows fed exclusively on grass and hay. It's generally aged longer than **grana padano** which is produced in other parts of Italy such as Piedmont, Lombardy, Veneto, Trentino and Romagna. Grana padano is also made from the milk of cows which are raised on grains, supplements and grass.

Pecorino is the generic Italian name for all cheese made from sheep milk. It's a hard, white to pale yellow cheese, traditionally made from November to June when sheep are grazing on natural pastures. Pecorino is usually matured for eight to 12 months and known for the region in which it's produced – Romano from Rome, Sardo from Sardinia, Siciliano from Sicily and Toscano from Tuscany. **Pepato** is a pecorino variety studded with black peppercorns.

Romano Originally pecorino romano, this hard sheep milk cheese has been made in the countryside around Rome since the 1st century. Widely exported since that time because of its excellent keeping qualities, romano is now made in other parts of the world from cow milk. Straw-coloured and grainy in texture, it's almost always used grated.

Ricotta The name for this soft, white, cow milk cheese roughly translates as "re-cooked". It's made from whey, a by-product of other cheesemaking, to which fresh milk and an acidic agent are added. Ricotta is a sweet, low-fat, moist cheese with a slightly grainy texture.

fetta

bocconcini

gorgonzola

ricotta

brie

mascarpone

vegetables and herbs

Start with the freshest seasonal produce your greengrocer has to offer, marry it with the pasta of your choice and a sprinkling of fresh herbs, and you'll be surprised how satisfying and delicious a meatless dish can be.

bow ties with zucchini in lemon garlic sauce

PREPARATION TIME 10 MINUTES • COOKING TIME 20 MINUTES

375g bow ties
3 medium yellow zucchini (360g)
3 medium green zucchini (360g)
30g butter
1 tablespoon olive oil
2 cloves garlic, crushed
1/3 cup (80ml) vegetable stock
1/2 cup (125ml) cream
2 teaspoons finely grated lemon rind
1/3 cup coarsely chopped fresh chives

1 Cook pasta in large saucepan of boiling water, uncovered, until just tender; drain.

2 While pasta is cooking, halve zucchini lengthways; slice halves thinly on the diagonal.

3 Heat butter and oil in large frying pan; cook zucchini and garlic over high heat, stirring, until zucchini is just tender. Add stock; bring to a boil. Reduce heat, add cream, rind and chives; stir until hot.

4 Place pasta in pan with zucchini sauce; toss gently to combine.

SERVES 4

per serving 26.1g fat; 2356kJ

pasta primavera

PREPARATION TIME 15 MINUTES • COOKING TIME 15 MINUTES

375g small spirals
1 tablespoon olive oil
1 medium brown onion (150g),
    chopped finely
3 cloves garlic, crushed
300g yellow patty-pan
    squash, quartered
1 medium red capsicum (200g),
    sliced thinly
200g sugar snap peas
1 medium carrot (120g),
    cut into ribbons
300ml cream
1 tablespoon seeded mustard
2 tablespoons coarsely chopped
    fresh flat-leaf parsley

1 Cook pasta in large saucepan of boiling water, uncovered, until just tender; drain.

2 While pasta is cooking, heat oil in large saucepan; cook onion and garlic, stirring, until onion softens. Add squash; cook, stirring, until just tender. Add capsicum, peas and carrot; cook, stirring, until capsicum is just tender.

3 Place pasta in pan with vegetables, add combined remaining ingredients; stir over low heat until just hot.

SERVES 4

per serving 38.9g fat; 3033kJ

pasta with chilli and leek

PREPARATION TIME 10 MINUTES • COOKING TIME 15 MINUTES

*Traditionally made with pancetta or prosciutto, our version of this Roman classic uses bacon,
taking a few liberties that make it easier to prepare and easier on the budget.*

4 (280g) rashers bacon,
    chopped coarsely
375g bucatini
80g butter
2 small leeks (400g),
    sliced thinly
2 cloves garlic, crushed
2 red thai chillies, chopped finely
6 green onions, chopped finely
1/2 cup (40g) finely grated
    parmesan cheese

1 Cook bacon in large heated dry frying pan, stirring, until browned; drain on absorbent paper.

2 Cook pasta in large saucepan of boiling water, uncovered, until just tender; drain.

3 While pasta is cooking, melt butter in medium frying pan; cook leek and garlic, stirring, about 5 minutes or until leek softens. Add bacon, chilli and onion; cook, stirring, 2 minutes or until onion softens.

4 Place pasta in large bowl with leek mixture and cheese; toss gently to combine.

SERVES 4

per serving 24.2g fat; 2441kJ
tip For a milder version, remove seeds from the chillies.

agnolotti in sage and pumpkin puree

PREPARATION TIME 15 MINUTES • COOKING TIME 15 MINUTES

Similar to ravioli, agnolotti are tiny pillows of pasta stuffed with one of any manner of different fillings. You can buy these already made, sold in cryovac packages, in the refrigerated section of your supermarket or fresh from specialty pasta makers.

1 teaspoon olive oil
1 small leek (200g), chopped finely
2 cloves garlic, crushed
400g peeled pumpkin, chopped
1/2 cup (125ml) buttermilk
1/2 cup (125ml) cream
1/2 cup (125ml) vegetable stock
750g ricotta and spinach agnolotti
vegetable oil, for shallow-frying
1 cup loosely packed fresh sage leaves
2 egg yolks, beaten slightly
1/4 cup (20g) finely grated parmesan cheese

1 Heat olive oil in large frying pan; cook leek and garlic, stirring, until leek softens.

2 Boil, steam or microwave pumpkin until tender, drain; blend or process, in batches, with buttermilk, cream and stock. Add pumpkin mixture to leek mixture; bring to a boil. Reduce heat; simmer, stirring, about 10 minutes or until mixture slightly thickens.

3 Meanwhile, cook pasta in large saucepan of boiling water, uncovered, until just tender; drain.

4 While pasta is cooking, heat vegetable oil in small frying pan; shallow-fry sage until crisp, drain on absorbent paper.

5 Stir egg yolks and cheese into pumpkin mixture; place in large bowl with pasta, toss gently to combine. Crumble fried sage leaves; sprinkle over pasta.

SERVES 4

per serving 28.6g fat; 2472kJ

spaghetti napoletana

PREPARATION TIME 5 MINUTES • COOKING TIME 25 MINUTES

2 teaspoons olive oil
1 small brown onion (80g), chopped finely
3 cloves garlic, crushed
3 x 415g cans whole peeled tomatoes
1/4 cup coarsely chopped, firmly packed fresh basil leaves
1/3 cup coarsely chopped, firmly packed fresh flat-leaf parsley
375g spaghetti

1 Heat oil in medium saucepan; cook onion and garlic, stirring, until onion softens.

2 Add undrained crushed tomatoes; bring to a boil. Reduce heat; simmer, uncovered, about 20 minutes or until reduced by about a third. Stir in basil and parsley.

3 Meanwhile, cook pasta in large saucepan of boiling water, uncovered, until just tender; drain. Serve pasta topped with sauce.

SERVES 4

per serving 4g fat; 1666kJ

tip If you cook this sauce even longer, until it is reduced by half, it makes a good pizza-base sauce or, with capers stirred through it, a delicious topping for chicken or veal scaloppine.

pasta with peas and prosciutto

PREPARATION TIME 5 MINUTES • COOKING TIME 15 MINUTES

1 tablespoon olive oil
1 large brown onion (200g),
 sliced thickly
1 clove garlic, crushed
6 slices prosciutto (100g),
 chopped coarsely
600ml bottled tomato
 pasta sauce
¹/₂ cup (125ml) cream
2 cups (250g) frozen peas
250g curly lasagne

1 Heat oil in large saucepan; cook onion, garlic and prosciutto, stirring, until onion softens. Add sauce, cream and peas; bring to a boil. Reduce heat; simmer, uncovered, until sauce thickens slightly.

2 Meanwhile, cook pasta in large saucepan of boiling water, uncovered, until just tender; drain.

3 Place pasta in large bowl with sauce; toss gently to combine.

SERVES 4

per serving 20.8g fat; 2163kJ

pagli e fieno

PREPARATION TIME 10 MINUTES • COOKING TIME 15 MINUTES

"Straw and hay" is how the name of this Parma favourite translates, so called because of the mixture

of plain and spinach-flavoured fettuccine tossed in its creamy mushroom sauce.

2 teaspoons olive oil
5 green onions, sliced thinly
2 cloves garlic, crushed
500g button mushrooms,
   sliced thickly
1 tablespoon dry white wine
300ml cream
¹⁄4 cup coarsely chopped fresh
   flat-leaf parsley
150g plain fettuccine
150g spinach-flavoured fettuccine

1 Heat oil in medium saucepan; cook onion and garlic, stirring, until onion softens.

2 Add mushrooms; cook, stirring, until just browned. Add wine and cream; bring to a boil. Reduce heat; simmer, uncovered, about 5 minutes or until sauce thickens slightly. Stir in parsley.

3 Meanwhile, cook both pastas in large saucepan of boiling water, uncovered, until just tender; drain. Place pasta in large bowl with sauce; toss gently to combine.

SERVES 4

per serving 36g fat; 2339kJ

minestrone on the run

PREPARATION TIME 10 MINUTES • COOKING TIME 25 MINUTES

1 tablespoon olive oil
1 medium brown onion (150g), chopped finely
2 cloves garlic, crushed
1 large carrot (180g), chopped coarsely
3 trimmed celery sticks (225g), chopped coarsely
2 medium parsnips (250g), chopped coarsely
2 x 415g cans whole peeled tomatoes
2 tablespoons tomato paste
3 cups (750ml) vegetable stock
1 1/2 cups (375ml) water
180g small macaroni
400g can borlotti beans, drained, rinsed
1/4 cup loosely packed, coarsely chopped fresh basil leaves
1/3 cup (25g) finely grated pecorino cheese

1 Heat oil in large saucepan; cook onion and garlic, stirring, until onion softens. Add carrot, celery and parsnip; cook, stirring, 5 minutes. Add undrained crushed tomatoes, paste, stock and the water, bring to a boil; cook, uncovered, 5 minutes.

2 Add pasta; boil, uncovered, until pasta is just tender.

3 Add beans; stir over low heat until hot. Stir in basil then serve minestrone sprinkled with cheese.

SERVES 4

per serving 8.7g fat; 1798kJ

tip Drained canned cannellini beans (or even chickpeas) can be substituted for borlotti beans.

penne, roast capsicum and baby vegetables in burnt butter sauce

PREPARATION TIME 15 MINUTES • COOKING TIME 20 MINUTES

2 medium red capsicums (400g)
375g penne
200g baby corn, halved lengthways
200g green beans, trimmed
100g butter
2 cloves garlic, crushed
2 tablespoons coarsely chopped fresh oregano

1 Quarter capsicums, remove and discard seeds and membranes. Roast under grill or in very hot oven, skin-side up, until skin blisters and blackens. Cover capsicum pieces with plastic or paper for 5 minutes, peel away skin, slice capsicum thinly.

2 Cook pasta in large saucepan of boiling water, uncovered, until just tender; drain.

3 While pasta is cooking, boil, steam or microwave corn and beans, separately, until just tender; drain. Melt butter in small saucepan; cook, stirring, about 3 minutes or until browned. Remove from heat; stir in garlic and oregano.

4 Place pasta in large bowl with corn, beans, capsicum and herbed burnt butter; toss gently to combine.

SERVES 4

per serving 22.4g fat; 2400kJ

tips Basil can be substituted for the oregano.

Capsicum can be roasted the day ahead and kept, covered, in the refrigerator.

mixed-mushroom orecchiette

PREPARATION TIME 10 MINUTES • COOKING TIME 15 MINUTES

1 tablespoon olive oil
1 medium brown onion (150g),
** chopped finely**
2 cloves garlic, crushed
250g button mushrooms,
** sliced thickly**
250g swiss brown mushrooms,
** sliced thickly**
250g flat mushrooms,
** sliced thickly**
250g spreadable cream cheese
¹/₂ cup (125ml) chicken stock
375g orecchiette
¹/₂ teaspoon cracked black pepper
2 tablespoons coarsely chopped
** fresh flat-leaf parsley**

1 Heat oil in large frying pan; cook onion and garlic, stirring, until onion softens. Add mushrooms; cook, stirring, until browned and tender. Add cream cheese and stock; cook over low heat, stirring, until cheese melts and mixture is hot.

2 Meanwhile, cook pasta in large saucepan of boiling water, uncovered, until just tender; drain. Place pasta in pan with mushroom sauce; stir in pepper and parsley, toss gently to combine.

SERVES 4

per serving 26.9g fat; 2615kJ

risoni with spinach and semi-dried tomatoes

PREPARATION TIME 5 MINUTES • COOKING TIME 25 MINUTES

30g butter
2 medium brown onions (300g), chopped finely
3 cloves garlic, crushed
500g risoni
4 cups (1 litre) chicken stock
1/2 cup (125ml) dry white wine
150g semi-dried tomatoes, halved
100g baby spinach leaves
1/3 cup (25g) finely grated parmesan cheese

1 Melt butter in large saucepan; cook onion and garlic, stirring, until onion softens. Add risoni; stir to coat in butter mixture. Stir in stock and wine; bring to a boil.

2 Reduce heat; simmer over medium heat, stirring, until liquid is absorbed and risoni is just tender. Gently stir in tomato, spinach and cheese.

SERVES 4

per serving 12.5g fat; 2777kJ

fettuccine with rocket pesto and fresh tomato salsa

PREPARATION TIME 10 MINUTES • COOKING TIME 15 MINUTES

500g fettuccine pasta
8 cloves garlic, quartered
½ cup coarsely chopped fresh basil
120g rocket, chopped coarsely
⅔ cup (160ml) olive oil
½ cup (40g) finely grated parmesan cheese
3 medium tomatoes (570g), chopped coarsely
2 tablespoons lemon juice
2 fresh small red thai chillies, sliced thinly
⅓ cup (50g) pine nuts, toasted

1 Cook pasta in large saucepan of boiling water, uncovered, until just tender; drain.

2 Meanwhile, blend or process garlic, basil, rocket and oil until smooth.

3 Combine pasta, rocket pesto, cheese, tomato, juice and chilli in large saucepan; cook, stirring, until hot. Add nuts; toss gently to combine.

SERVES 4

per serving 50.3g fat; 3780kJ (904 cal)
tip You could substitute baby spinach leaves for the rocket for a milder pesto.

herbed artichoke and tomato sauce with spirals

PREPARATION TIME 10 MINUTES • COOKING TIME 20 MINUTES

2 teaspoons olive oil
1 medium brown onion (150g), chopped finely
2 cloves garlic, crushed
3 x 415g cans peeled tomato pieces
1 tablespoon coarsely chopped fresh oregano
1/3 cup loosely packed, coarsely chopped fresh basil leaves
375g large spirals
400g can artichoke hearts, drained, quartered
1/2 cup (40g) finely grated parmesan cheese

1 Heat oil in large saucepan; cook onion and garlic, stirring, until onion softens. Add undrained tomatoes; bring to a boil. Reduce heat, add oregano and basil; simmer, uncovered, about 10 minutes or until sauce reduces by a third.

2 Meanwhile, cook pasta in large saucepan of boiling water, uncovered, until just tender; drain.

3 Place pasta, artichoke pieces and half of the cheese in pan with tomato sauce; toss gently to combine, serve with remaining cheese.

SERVES 4

per serving 7.5g fat; 1916kJ

linguine al pesto

PREPARATION TIME 15 MINUTES • COOKING TIME 12 MINUTES

2 cups firmly packed fresh basil leaves
2 cloves garlic, peeled, quartered
1/2 cup (40g) coarsely grated parmesan cheese
1/3 cup (50g) toasted pine nuts
1/2 cup (125ml) olive oil
375g linguine

1 Blend or process basil, garlic, cheese and nuts with a little of the olive oil. When basil mixture is just pureed, gradually pour in remaining oil with motor operating; blend until mixture forms a paste.

2 Cook pasta in large saucepan of boiling water, uncovered, until just tender; drain. Combine pasta in large bowl with pesto; toss gently.

SERVES 4

per serving 41.6g fat; 2617kJ

tip Pesto freezes well so it will see you through the winter if you make several quantities of this recipe when basil is in season. Freeze in ice-cube trays, covered tightly, or individual snap-lock freezer bags. One cube of frozen pesto can be stirred into homemade minestrone or tomato soup to add a piquant taste.

eggplant pasta sauce

PREPARATION TIME 10 MINUTES • COOKING TIME 20 MINUTES

1/4 cup (60ml) olive oil
1 medium brown onion (150g), chopped finely
2 trimmed celery sticks (150g), chopped finely
1 clove garlic, crushed
2 tablespoons brandy
1 medium eggplant (300g), sliced thinly
600ml bottled tomato pasta sauce
1/2 cup (140g) tomato paste
1/2 cup (125ml) water
375g rigatoni
1/4 cup (20g) finely grated parmesan cheese

1 Heat oil in large saucepan; cook onion, celery and garlic, stirring, until onion softens. Add brandy; cook, stirring, until brandy evaporates. Add eggplant; cook, stirring, until eggplant is tender.

2 Stir in sauce, paste and the water; bring to a boil. Reduce heat; simmer, uncovered, about 10 minutes or until sauce thickens slightly.

3 Meanwhile, cook pasta in large saucepan of boiling water, uncovered, until just tender; drain. Place pasta in large bowl with half of the eggplant sauce; toss gently to combine. Divide pasta among serving plates; top each with remaining sauce and cheese.

SERVES 4

per serving 16.9g fat; 2420kJ

penne arrabiata

PREPARATION TIME 10 MINUTES • COOKING TIME 15 MINUTES

1 tablespoon olive oil
2 medium brown onions (300g),
chopped finely
5 cloves garlic, crushed
3 red thai chillies, chopped finely
600ml bottled tomato pasta sauce
2 teaspoons balsamic vinegar
375g penne
1/4 cup (20g) finely grated
parmesan cheese

1 Heat oil in large saucepan; cook onion, garlic and chilli, stirring, until onion softens. Add sauce and vinegar; bring to a boil. Reduce heat; simmer, uncovered, about 5 minutes or until sauce thickens slightly.

2 Meanwhile, cook pasta in large saucepan of boiling water, uncovered, until just tender; drain. Combine pasta with sauce; sprinkle with cheese.

SERVES 4

per serving 7.6g fat; 1904kJ

tagliatelle puttanesca

PREPARATION TIME 10 MINUTES • COOKING TIME 20 MINUTES

2 teaspoons vegetable oil
1 large brown onion (200g),
  sliced thickly
3 cloves garlic, crushed
4 red thai chillies, seeded,
  chopped finely
600ml bottled tomato pasta sauce
1/4 cup (40g) drained capers
1 cup (160g) kalamata
  olives, seeded
8 drained anchovies, halved
1/2 cup coarsely chopped fresh
  flat-leaf parsley
375g tagliatelle

1 Heat oil in large frying pan; cook onion, garlic and chilli, stirring, until onion softens. Add sauce, capers, olives and anchovies; bring to a boil. Reduce heat; simmer, uncovered, about 5 minutes or until sauce thickens slightly. Stir in parsley.

2 Cook pasta in large saucepan of boiling water, uncovered, until just tender; drain. Serve pasta with sauce.

SERVES 4

per serving 4.7g fat; 1902kJ

pesto & tapenade

Transform a bowl of just-cooked pasta into an instant feast simply by keeping supplies of these intensely savoury condiments in your fridge or freezer. They will keep in the refrigerator for at least a week; cover with a film of oil to stop oxygen getting to the paste. If you want to keep them longer, spoon into a sealable container and freeze. Because of their high oil content, they never freeze quite solid – so you can extract a single spoonful without defrosting the whole amount. Try dropping a spoonful into a meat gravy, a pot of vegetable soup or beaten eggs for an omelette to find out how versatile these piquant mixtures can be.

mint pistachio pesto

1 cup firmly packed fresh mint leaves
1/3 cup (50g) pistachios, toasted
1/3 cup (25g) coarsely grated parmesan cheese
2 cloves garlic, quartered
1 tablespoon lemon juice
1/4 cup (60ml) olive oil
2 tablespoons water, approximately

Blend or process mint, nuts, cheese, garlic and juice until almost smooth. With motor operating, gradually add oil and just enough water to give pesto desired consistency.

MAKES 1 CUP (220g)

per tablespoon 8.6g fat; 343kJ

spinach walnut pesto

250g baby spinach leaves, trimmed
1/2 cup (50g) walnut pieces, toasted
1 clove garlic, quartered
1/4 cup (20g) coarsely grated parmesan cheese
2 tablespoons lemon juice
1/2 cup (125ml) extra virgin olive oil

Blend or process spinach, nuts, garlic, cheese and juice until almost smooth; with motor operating, gradually add oil until pesto is of desired consistency.

MAKES 1 1/2 CUPS (380g)

per tablespoon 8.6g fat; 343kJ

cashew, coriander and mint pesto

You need approximately four bunches of fresh coriander to make this recipe.

3/4 cup (110g) raw cashews, toasted
4 cups (approximately 250g) firmly packed fresh coriander leaves
1/2 cup firmly packed fresh mint leaves
1/3 cup (80ml) lime juice
1/2 cup (125ml) extra virgin olive oil

Blend or process cashews, coriander, mint and juice until well combined. With motor operating, gradually add oil until pesto is of desired consistency.

MAKES 2 CUPS (510g)

per tablespoon 7g fat; 294kJ

traditional tapenade

1 tablespoon drained capers
3 anchovy fillets, drained
1/2 cup (60g) seeded black olives
1/4 cup (60ml) extra virgin olive oil

Blend or process combined ingredients
until pesto is of desired consistency.

MAKES 1/2 CUP (125g)

per tablespoon 9.4g fat; 399kJ

coriander pesto

2 tablespoons unsalted roasted peanuts
1/2 cup firmly packed fresh coriander leaves
2 cloves garlic, quartered
1/2 cup (125ml) peanut oil

Blend or process combined ingredients until smooth.

MAKES 2/3 CUP (175g)

per tablespoon 15.6g fat; 597kJ

sun-dried tomato and olive tapenade

1 cup (150g) drained sun-dried tomatoes in oil
1/3 cup (80ml) extra virgin olive oil
2 tablespoons red wine vinegar
1 tablespoon brown sugar
1 tablespoon coarsely chopped fresh oregano
1 tablespoon coarsely chopped fresh basil leaves
1/2 teaspoon cracked black peppercorns
2/3 cup (70g) pecans, toasted
1/3 cup (50g) seeded black olives

Blend or process ingredients until smooth.

MAKES 11/3 CUPS (330g)

per tablespoon 10.4g fat; 496kJ

meat and poultry

Exploit pasta's great versatility with these recipes that call for veal, chicken, ham, beef or lamb as their basis and an enlivening array of multicultural influences as their inspiration.

penne with chile con carne

PREPARATION TIME 8 MINUTES • COOKING TIME 20 MINUTES

375g penne
1 tablespoon peanut oil
1 large brown onion (200g),
  sliced thinly
2 cloves garlic, crushed
2 small red thai chillies, seeded,
  chopped coarsely
1 teaspoon ground cumin
1 teaspoon ground coriander
350g yellow teardrop
  tomatoes, halved
500g thinly sliced roast beef
420g can kidney beans,
  drained, rinsed
600ml bottled tomato pasta sauce
1/3 cup loosely packed fresh
  coriander leaves

1 Cook pasta in large saucepan of boiling water, uncovered, until just tender; drain.

2 While pasta is cooking, heat oil in large saucepan; cook onion, garlic, chilli and ground spices, stirring, until onion softens. Add tomato; cook, stirring, until tomato is just soft. Add beef, beans and sauce; bring to a boil. Reduce heat; simmer, uncovered, until sauce thickens slightly.

3 Place pasta in pan with chile con carne; toss gently over heat until combined and hot. Stir in fresh coriander.

SERVES 4

per serving 12.1g fat; 2853kJ

orecchiette with ham, artichokes and sun-dried tomatoes

PREPARATION TIME 10 MINUTES • COOKING TIME 15 MINUTES

If you can find fresh orecchiette (little ears), use them instead of the packaged dried version.

375g orecchiette
500g leg ham, sliced thickly
340g jar artichoke hearts in oil,
   drained, quartered
1/2 cup (75g) sun-dried
   tomatoes, halved
1 cup (80g) flaked
   parmesan cheese
1 cup loosely packed fresh
   flat-leaf parsley
2 tablespoons lemon juice
1 tablespoon seeded mustard
1 tablespoon honey
1 clove garlic, crushed
1/2 cup (125ml) olive oil

1 Cook pasta in large saucepan of boiling water, uncovered, until just tender; drain.

2 Place pasta in large bowl with ham, artichoke, tomato, cheese, parsley and combined remaining ingredients; toss gently to combine.

SERVES 4

per serving 46.1g fat; 3771kJ

chicken and fennel spirals

PREPARATION TIME 10 MINUTES • COOKING TIME 20 MINUTES

2 medium fennel bulbs (1kg),
   trimmed, sliced thinly
3 cloves garlic, sliced thinly
1/4 cup (60ml) dry sherry
1 1/2 cups (375ml) chicken stock
375g large spirals
2 cups (340g) shredded
   cooked chicken
200g snow peas, trimmed,
   sliced thinly
1 cup (240g) sour cream
1 tablespoon coarsely chopped
   fresh tarragon

1 Preheat oven to very hot.

2 Combine fennel, garlic, sherry and 1/2 cup of the stock in large baking dish; roast, uncovered, in very hot oven about 15 minutes or until fennel is just tender.

3 Cook pasta in large saucepan of boiling water, uncovered, until just tender; drain.

4 Place fennel mixture and pasta in same cleaned pan with remaining ingredients; stir over low heat until hot.

SERVES 4

per serving 31.5g fat; 3106kJ

bucatini with moroccan lamb sauce

PREPARATION TIME 10 MINUTES • COOKING TIME 20 MINUTES

2 teaspoons olive oil
1 small brown onion (80g), chopped finely
2 cloves garlic, crushed
500g minced lamb
1 teaspoon ground cumin
1/2 teaspoon ground cayenne pepper
1/2 teaspoon ground cinnamon
2 tablespoons tomato paste
2 x 415g cans tomatoes
1 large green zucchini (150g), chopped coarsely
2 tablespoons finely chopped fresh mint leaves
375g bucatini

1 Heat oil in large saucepan; cook onion and garlic, stirring, until onion softens. Add lamb; cook, stirring, until changed in colour. Add spices; cook, stirring, until fragrant.

2 Stir in paste, undrained crushed tomatoes and zucchini; bring to a boil. Reduce heat; simmer, uncovered, about 15 minutes or until sauce thickens slightly. Stir in mint.

3 Meanwhile, cook pasta in large saucepan of boiling water, uncovered, until just tender; drain. Serve pasta topped with sauce.

SERVES 4

per serving 11.9g fat; 2357kJ

chicken liver sauce with curly lasagne

PREPARATION TIME 10 MINUTES • COOKING TIME 20 MINUTES

This is our variation of the classic Italian sauce called fegatini di pollo, and is one for those of you who adore the sweet tenderness of chicken livers. Be sure not to overcook them or they will be dry and unappealing.

500g chicken livers
1/2 cup (50g) packaged breadcrumbs
1/4 cup (60ml) olive oil
1 medium brown onion (150g), chopped coarsely
4 medium tomatoes (520g), chopped coarsely
1/2 cup (125ml) chicken stock
1/4 cup (60ml) balsamic vinegar
1/4 cup (60ml) dry red wine
2 tablespoons coarsely chopped fresh rosemary
375g curly lasagne

1 Halve each trimmed chicken liver lobe; toss in breadcrumbs, shaking off excess. Heat half of the oil in large frying pan; cook liver over high heat, in batches, until browned and cooked as desired.

2 Heat remaining oil in same pan; cook onion, stirring, until soft. Add tomato; cook, stirring, until tomato is pulpy. Add stock, vinegar, wine and rosemary to pan; cook, stirring, until sauce thickens slightly.

3 Meanwhile, cook pasta in large saucepan of boiling water, uncovered, until just tender; drain. Stir pasta and liver into tomato sauce; toss gently to combine.

SERVES 4

per serving 20.3g fat; 2765kJ

penne with lamb and roasted capsicum

PREPARATION TIME 10 MINUTES • COOKING TIME 15 MINUTES

3 large red capsicums (1kg)
500g lamb fillets
2 tablespoons olive oil
2 teaspoons ground cumin
2 x 415g cans tomato puree
1/2 cup (60g) drained semi-dried
  tomatoes, chopped coarsely
375g penne
1/4 cup finely shredded fresh
  basil leaves

1 Quarter capsicums, remove seeds and membranes. Place capsicum on oven tray, skin-side up; roast under heated grill or in very hot oven until skin blisters and blackens. Cover capsicum pieces with plastic or paper for 5 minutes; peel away skin, then slice capsicum pieces thinly.

2 Combine lamb, oil and cumin in medium bowl; cook lamb, in batches, in large heated oiled frying pan (or grill or barbecue) until browned all over and cooked as desired. Stand 5 minutes; cut into thin slices.

3 Heat large frying pan; add puree, tomato and capsicum; bring to a boil. Reduce heat; simmer, uncovered, about 5 minutes or until sauce thickens slightly.

4 Meanwhile, cook pasta in large saucepan of boiling water, uncovered, until just tender; drain. Place pasta in large bowl with lamb, tomato sauce and basil; toss gently to combine.

SERVES 4

per serving 12.8g fat; 2747kJ

macaroni with beef sausages

PREPARATION TIME 10 MINUTES • COOKING TIME 20 MINUTES

400g thin beef sausages
600ml bottled tomato pasta sauce
4 trimmed celery sticks (300g),
chopped coarsely
1 medium green capsicum (200g),
chopped coarsely
250g elbow macaroni
2 tablespoons finely chopped
fresh basil leaves
1 cup (100g) coarsely grated
mozzarella cheese

1 Cook sausages, in batches, in large heated frying pan until browned all over and cooked through; drain on absorbent paper, cut into 1cm slices.

2 Place sauce in same cleaned pan; bring to a boil. Add sausage, celery and capsicum; cook, stirring occasionally, about 5 minutes or until vegetables are just tender.

3 Meanwhile, cook pasta in large saucepan of boiling water, uncovered, until just tender; drain.

4 Place pasta, basil and cheese in pan with sausage and tomato sauce; toss gently to combine.

SERVES 4

per serving 31.9g fat; 2644kJ

tip Try making this recipe with some of the more exotic sausages so readily available these days (one variety with fennel and chilli is especially delicious when cooked in tomato sauce).

tagliatelle, chicken and peas in mustard cream sauce

PREPARATION TIME 15 MINUTES • COOKING TIME 15 MINUTES

250g tagliatelle
1 tablespoon olive oil
1 medium brown onion (150g), chopped finely
2 cloves garlic, crushed
1/2 cup (125ml) dry white wine
1 tablespoon dijon mustard
1 cup (250ml) cream
2 cups (250g) frozen peas, thawed
2 cups (340g) shredded cooked chicken
1/4 cup finely chopped fresh garlic chives

1 Cook pasta in large saucepan of boiling water, uncovered, until just tender; drain.

2 While pasta is cooking, heat oil in large saucepan; cook onion and garlic, stirring, until onion softens. Add wine and mustard; bring to a boil. Reduce heat; simmer, uncovered, 5 minutes. Stir in cream; return mixture to a boil, then simmer again, uncovered, about 5 minutes or until sauce thickens slightly. Stir in drained peas and chicken; stir over low heat until mixture is hot.

3 Place pasta and chives in pan with chicken and pea sauce; toss gently to combine.

SERVES 4

per serving 38.9g fat; 2999kJ

tip Skinned and boned leftover roast or barbecued chicken can be used in this recipe, as can poached chicken breast or thigh fillets.

linguine and chorizo in creamy mushroom sauce

PREPARATION TIME 10 MINUTES • COOKING TIME 20 MINUTES

300g swiss brown mushrooms, halved
2 tablespoons olive oil
2 cloves garlic, crushed
2 (400g) chorizo sausages
1/2 cup (125ml) dry white wine
1 cup (250ml) chicken stock
300g carton sour cream
4 green onions, chopped finely
375g linguine
2 tablespoons finely shredded fresh basil leaves

1 Preheat oven to very hot.

2 Place mushrooms in large shallow baking dish, drizzle with combined oil and garlic; roast, uncovered, in very hot oven about 15 minutes or until mushrooms are browned and tender.

3 Meanwhile, cook chorizo in heated medium frying pan until browned and cooked through; drain on absorbent paper, chop coarsely.

4 Place wine in same cleaned pan; bring to a boil. Reduce heat; simmer, uncovered, 5 minutes. Stir in stock and cream; return mixture to a boil. Reduce heat; simmer, uncovered, about 2 minutes or until sauce is hot. Remove sauce from heat; stir in mushrooms and onion.

5 Meanwhile, cook pasta in large saucepan of boiling water, uncovered, until just tender; drain. Place pasta in large bowl with mushroom sauce, chorizo and basil; toss gently to combine.

SERVES 4

per serving 70.5g fat; 4602kJ

tip Sprinkle finely grated parmesan cheese and coarsely ground black pepper over individual servings of this dish.

bow ties in chicken and cabbage sauce

PREPARATION TIME 10 MINUTES • COOKING TIME 25 MINUTES (plus standing time)

You need a small cabbage with an untrimmed weight of approximately 750g for this recipe.

1 tablespoon olive oil
340g chicken breast fillets
375g bow ties
1 medium brown onion (150g),
   sliced thinly
7¹/₂ cups (600g) finely
   shredded cabbage
1¹/₂ cups (375ml) chicken stock
400g can tomatoes
¹/₄ cup (70g) tomato paste
³/₄ cup (180ml) cream

1 Preheat oven to moderately hot.

2 Heat oil in large frying pan; cook chicken until browned all over. Place chicken on oven tray; bake, uncovered, in moderately hot oven about 10 minutes or until cooked through. Stand 5 minutes; slice thinly.

3 Cook pasta in large saucepan of boiling water, uncovered, until just tender; drain.

4 While pasta is cooking, cook onion, stirring, in same frying pan, until just soft. Add cabbage; cook, stirring, until cabbage is tender. Add stock, undrained crushed tomatoes and paste; bring mixture to a boil. Reduce heat; simmer, uncovered, about 5 minutes or until sauce thickens slightly. Stir in cream then chicken.

5 Add pasta to chicken mixture; toss gently to combine.

SERVES 4

per serving 30.7g fat; 3023kJ

spaghetti bolognese

PREPARATION TIME 5 MINUTES • COOKING TIME 30 MINUTES

1 tablespoon olive oil
2 cloves garlic, crushed
1 medium brown onion (150g),
    chopped finely
1 medium carrot (120g),
    chopped finely
2 trimmed celery sticks (150g),
    chopped finely
500g minced beef
1/2 cup (125ml) dry red wine
600ml bottled tomato pasta sauce
1 bay leaf
375g spaghetti
1/2 cup (40g) finely grated
    parmesan cheese

1 Heat oil in large saucepan; cook
   garlic, onion, carrot and celery,
   stirring, until onion softens.

2 Add beef; cook, stirring, until
   beef is cooked through. Add
   wine, sauce and bay leaf;
   boil, uncovered, about
   10 minutes or until sauce
   thickens. Remove and discard
   bay leaf.

3 Meanwhile, cook pasta in
   large saucepan of boiling
   water, uncovered, until just
   tender; drain.

4 Serve pasta topped with meat
   sauce and cheese.

SERVES 4
per serving 18.3g fat; 2620kJ

greek lamb, fetta and eggplant pasta

PREPARATION TIME 20 MINUTES • COOKING TIME 15 MINUTES

1 medium eggplant (300g), chopped coarsely
cooking salt
500g lamb fillets
2 tablespoons olive oil
250g large shells
1 medium red onion (170g), sliced
100g baby rocket leaves
2 medium tomatoes (380g), seeded, sliced thinly
¼ cup loosely packed fresh oregano leaves
200g fetta cheese, crumbled

BALSAMIC VINAIGRETTE
¼ cup (60ml) balsamic vinegar
½ cup (125ml) olive oil
2 cloves garlic, crushed
2 tablespoons seeded mustard

1 Place eggplant in colander, sprinkle all over with salt. Stand 5 minutes; rinse under cold water, drain on absorbent paper.

2 Meanwhile, cook lamb, in batches, in large non-stick frying pan until browned and cooked as desired. Stand 5 minutes; cut into thick slices.

3 Heat oil in same pan; cook eggplant, in batches, until browned all over and tender.

4 Meanwhile, cook pasta in large saucepan of boiling water, uncovered, until just tender; drain. Place pasta, lamb and eggplant in large bowl with remaining ingredients; drizzle with dressing, toss gently to combine.

balsamic vinaigrette Combine ingredients in screw-top jar; shake well.

SERVES 4

per serving 55.1g fat; 3636kJ

spaghetti and meatballs

PREPARATION TIME 15 MINUTES • COOKING TIME 20 MINUTES

500g pork mince
2 tablespoons coarsely chopped fresh flat-leaf parsley
1 clove garlic, crushed
1 egg
1 cup (70g) stale breadcrumbs
1 tablespoon tomato paste
2 tablespoons olive oil
400g can tomatoes
600ml bottled tomato pasta sauce
375g spaghetti
1/3 cup (25g) finely grated romano cheese

1 Combine pork, parsley, garlic, egg, breadcrumbs and paste in large bowl; roll tablespoons of pork mixture into balls. Heat oil in large saucepan; cook meatballs, in batches, until browned all over.

2 Place undrained crushed tomatoes and sauce in same pan; bring to a boil. Return meatballs to pan, reduce heat; simmer, uncovered, about 10 minutes or until meatballs are cooked through.

3 Meanwhile, cook pasta in large saucepan of boiling water, uncovered, until just tender; drain. Divide pasta among serving bowls; top with meatballs, sprinkle with cheese.

SERVES 4

per serving 23g fat; 3149kJ

tips Meatballs can be made and fried a day ahead; keep, covered, in the refrigerator until the sauce is made.

To save time when making the recipe on another occasion, double the meatball quantities and freeze half of them after frying. Thaw meatballs overnight in refrigerator before adding to the sauce.

fettuccine veal goulash

PREPARATION TIME 15 MINUTES • COOKING TIME 15 MINUTES

400g veal fillet
2 teaspoons olive oil
1 medium brown onion (150g), sliced finely
2 cloves garlic, crushed
1 teaspoon sweet paprika
1 1/2 cups (375ml) beef stock
2 tablespoons sour cream
1 tablespoon lemon juice
1 tablespoon seeded mustard
375g fettuccine
250g spinach, trimmed, shredded coarsely
1 tablespoon fresh dill tips

1 Cook veal, turning, in large heated frying pan until browned and cooked as desired. Stand 5 minutes; cut into thin slices, keep warm.

2 Heat oil in same pan; cook onion, garlic and paprika, stirring, until onion softens. Add stock; bring to a boil. Reduce heat; simmer, uncovered, 5 minutes. Add sour cream, juice and mustard; cook, stirring, 1 minute.

3 Meanwhile, cook pasta in large saucepan of boiling water, uncovered, until just tender; drain. Place pasta, spinach and dill in large bowl with veal goulash; toss gently to combine.

SERVES 4

per serving 10.2g fat; 2147kJ

tip Change the dill to tarragon and add a teaspoon of worcestershire sauce to make this dish similar to a traditional stroganoff in flavour.

pasta pronto

When you're simply famished and want to eat *now*, help is at hand with these faster-pasta recipes, each of which can be on the table in slightly more time than it takes to cook the pasta. Each recipe serves four people and you're likely to have most of the ingredients in your pantry or refrigerator.

roast tomato with basil and olive oil

Cook 375g pasta in large saucepan of boiling water, uncovered, until just tender; drain. Meanwhile, place 8 medium (600g) coarsely chopped egg tomatoes in large baking dish with 2 crushed garlic cloves and 1/4 cup (60ml) extra virgin olive oil; roast, uncovered, in hot oven about 10 minutes or until tomato softens and browns slightly. Combine tomato mixture in large bowl with pasta and 1/2 cup finely shredded fresh basil leaves; toss gently to combine.

per serving 14.9g fat; 1901kJ

garlic breadcrumbs and poached eggs

Cook 375g pasta in large saucepan of boiling water, uncovered, until just tender; drain. Meanwhile, heat 1/3 cup (80ml) olive oil in large heated frying pan; cook 2 crushed garlic cloves and 2 cups (140g) stale breadcrumbs, stirring, until breadcrumbs are browned. Combine pasta and breadcrumb mixture in large bowl with 2 cups (50g) baby rocket leaves; toss gently to combine. Divide pasta among serving plates; top each with a just-poached egg.

per serving 27g fat; 2892kJ

parsley and parmesan burnt butter

Cook 375g pasta in large saucepan of boiling water, uncovered, until just tender; drain. Meanwhile, melt 100g butter in medium frying pan; cook, stirring, over high heat until browned. Add 2 crushed garlic cloves and 1/2 cup firmly packed, coarsely chopped fresh flat-leaf parsley; cook, stirring, 1 minute. Combine burnt butter mixture and pasta in large bowl with 1 cup (80g) flaked parmesan cheese; toss gently to combine.

per serving 28.1g fat; 2444kJ

zucchini and lemon

Cook 375g pasta in large saucepan of boiling water, uncovered, until just tender; drain. Meanwhile, melt 100g butter in large saucepan; cook 4 medium (480g) coarsely grated zucchini and 1 crushed garlic clove, stirring, until zucchini is tender. Combine zucchini mixture and pasta in large bowl with 2 teaspoons finely grated lemon rind and 1 tablespoon lemon juice; toss gently to combine.

per serving 21.9g fat; 2148kJ

roast tomato with basil and olive oil

anchovy and garlic tomato sauce

Cook 375g pasta in large saucepan of boiling water, uncovered, until just tender; drain. Meanwhile, blend or process 8 drained anchovy fillets with 4 roughly chopped garlic cloves and 4 roughly chopped green onions until mixture forms a smooth paste. Place anchovy paste in large bowl with 2 cups (500ml) heated bottled tomato pasta sauce and pasta; toss gently to combine.

per serving 2g fat; 1572kJ

coriander pesto, parmesan and lemon juice

Cook 375g pasta in large saucepan of boiling water, uncovered, until just tender; drain. Combine pasta in large bowl with 2 tablespoons olive oil, 1/2 cup (130g) bottled coriander pesto, 2 tablespoons lemon juice and 1/2 cup (40g) finely grated parmesan cheese; toss gently to combine. Sprinkle with 1/4 cup (40g) toasted pine nuts.

per serving 29.5g fat; 2561kJ

garlic, chilli and parmesan

Cook 375g pasta in large saucepan of boiling water, uncovered, until just tender; drain. Combine pasta in large bowl with 3 seeded, finely sliced red thai chillies, 2 crushed garlic cloves, 1/2 cup (40g) flaked parmesan cheese, 1/4 cup firmly packed, coarsely chopped fresh flat-leaf parsley and 1/4 cup (60ml) olive oil; toss to combine.

per serving 18g fat; 2001kJ

seafood

Seafood is perfect with all types of pasta. Its fresh, clean taste and quick cooking time make it a great starter or light main course. Parmesan is not usually served with seafood pasta, but it's a matter of personal taste.

scallops with asparagus

PREPARATION TIME 5 MINUTES • COOKING TIME 20 MINUTES

375g large spirals
2 teaspoons olive oil
500g asparagus, trimmed,
   cut into 5cm lengths
400g scallops
1 cup (250ml) dry white wine
300ml cream
2 tablespoons fresh dill tips
1 tablespoon finely shredded
   lemon rind
1 tablespoon lemon juice

1 Cook pasta in large saucepan of boiling water, uncovered, until just tender; drain.

2 While pasta is cooking, heat half of the oil in large frying pan; cook asparagus, in batches, stirring, until just tender.

3 Heat remaining oil in same pan; cook scallops, in batches, until browned both sides. Add wine to same pan; boil, uncovered, until reduced by three-quarters. Reduce heat, add cream; simmer, uncovered, until sauce thickens slightly.

4 Place pasta in pan with asparagus, scallops and remaining ingredients; toss gently over low heat until hot.

SERVES 4

per serving 36.9g fat; 3139kJ

spaghetti marinara

PREPARATION TIME 5 MINUTES • COOKING TIME 15 MINUTES

1 tablespoon olive oil
1 medium brown onion (150g),
  chopped finely
1/3 cup (80ml) dry white wine
1/3 cup (95g) tomato paste
2 x 425g cans whole
  peeled tomatoes
750g seafood marinara mix
1/4 cup loosely packed, coarsely
  chopped fresh flat-leaf parsley
375g spaghetti

1 Heat oil in large frying pan; cook onion, stirring, until soft.

2 Add wine, paste and undrained crushed tomatoes to pan; bring to a boil. Reduce heat; simmer, uncovered, for 10 minutes or until sauce thickens slightly.

3 Add marinara mix; cook, stirring occasionally, about 5 minutes or until seafood is cooked through. Stir in parsley.

4 Meanwhile, cook pasta in a large saucepan of boiling water, uncovered, until just tender; drain.

5 Serve marinara mixture on top of pasta.

SERVES 4

per serving 10.7g fat; 1932kJ

clear prawn and crushed noodle soup

PREPARATION TIME 10 MINUTES • COOKING TIME 15 MINUTES

500g medium uncooked prawns
150g tagliatelle, broken roughly
1.25 litres (5 cups) chicken stock
2 cups (500ml) water
20g piece fresh galangal,
  chopped finely
20g piece fresh ginger,
  chopped finely
4 kaffir lime leaves
1 tablespoon finely chopped
  lemon grass
1/3 cup (80ml) lemon juice
1/4 cup (60ml) fish sauce
1 tablespoon sambal oelek
1 red thai chilli, seeded,
  sliced thinly
1/4 cup loosely packed, coarsely
  chopped fresh coriander leaves

1 Shell and devein prawns, leaving tails intact.

2 Cook pasta in large saucepan of boiling water, uncovered, until just tender; drain.

3 While pasta is cooking, combine stock, the water, galangal, ginger, lime leaves and lemon grass in large saucepan; bring to a boil. Boil, uncovered, about 5 minutes or until reduced by a quarter. Add juice, sauce, sambal and prawns, reduce heat; cook, uncovered, until prawns just change in colour. Remove from heat; discard lime leaves, add chilli and coriander.

4 Divide pasta and prawn mixture among serving bowls; ladle soup over the top.

SERVES 4

per serving 2.3g fat; 974kJ

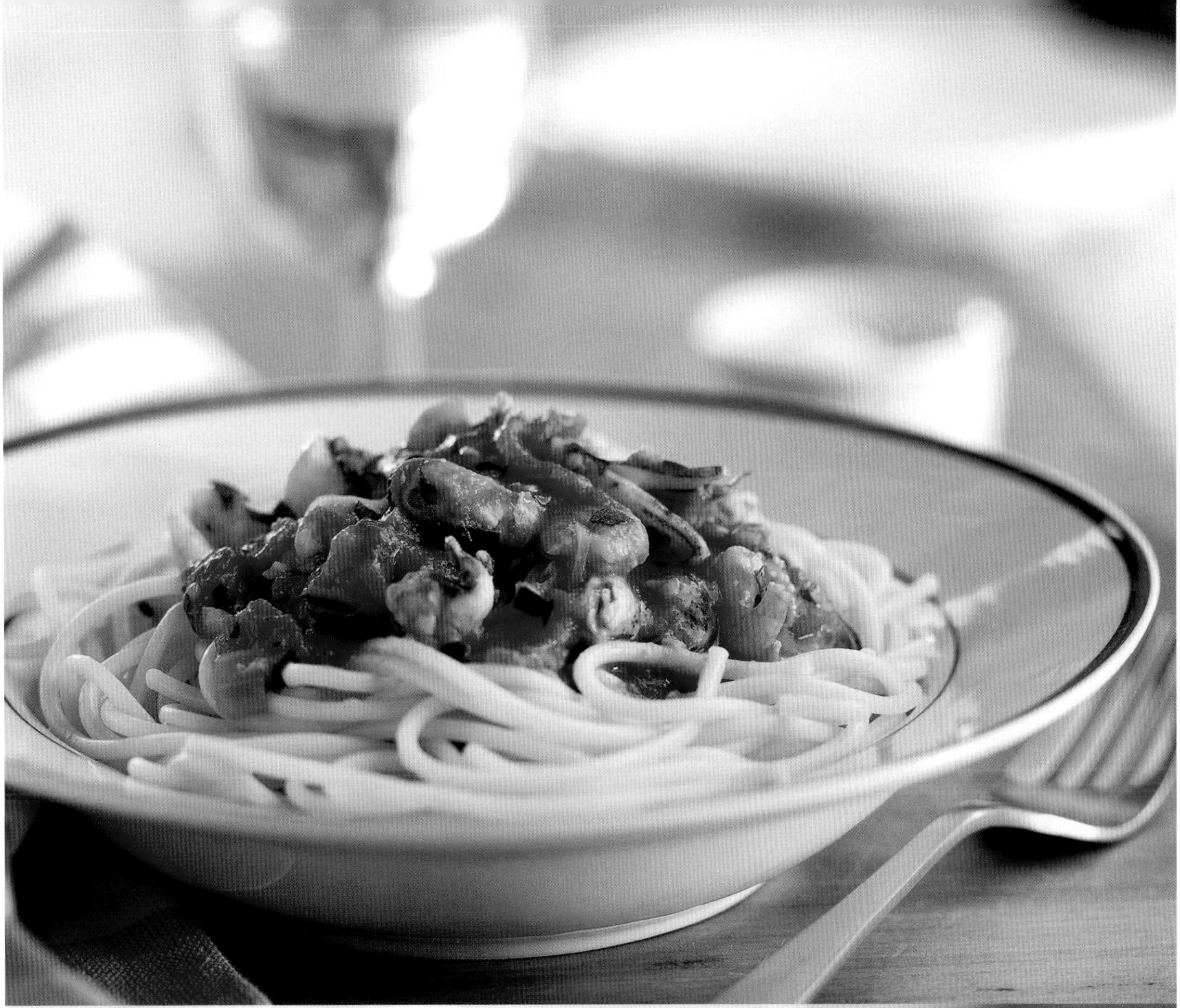

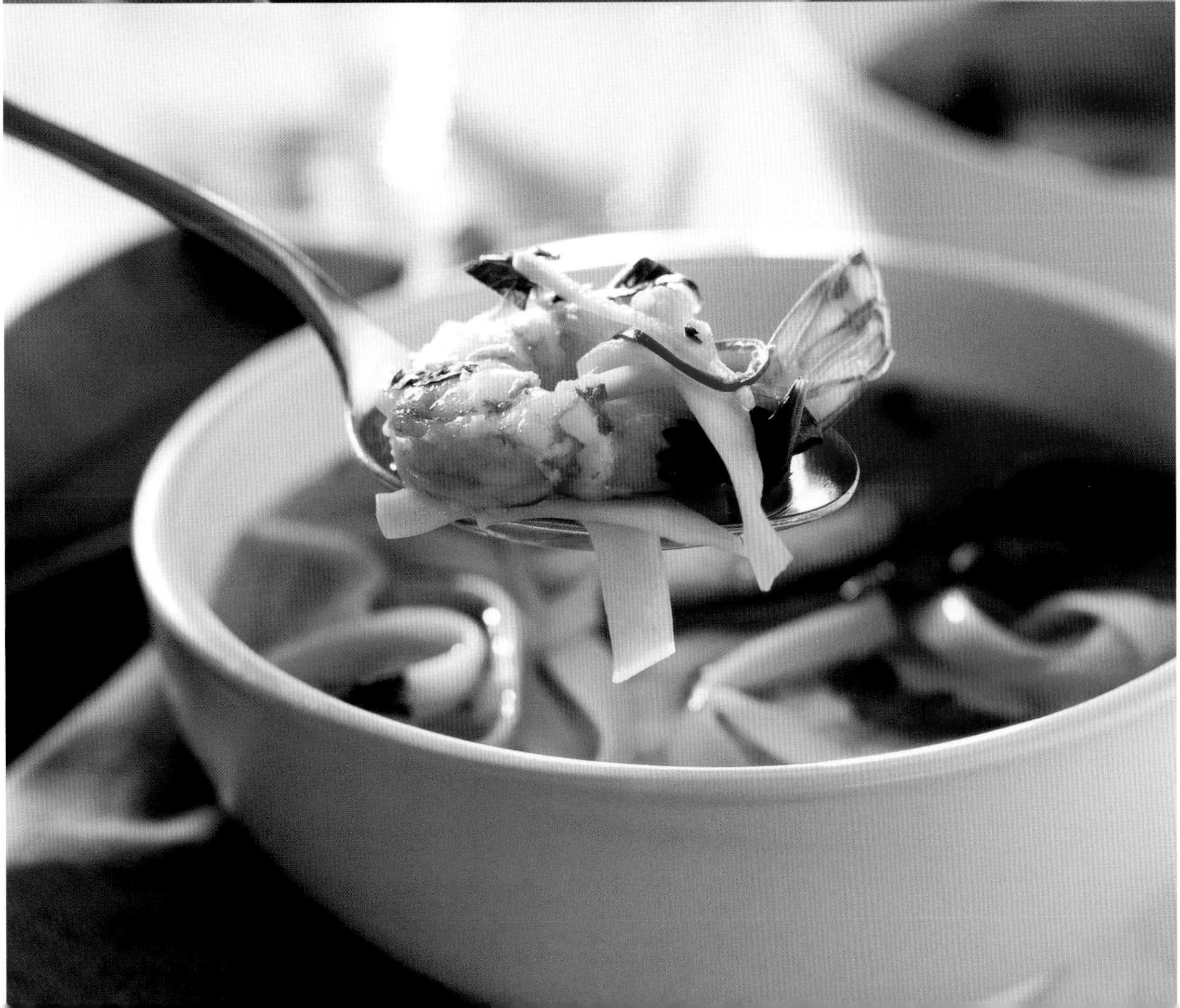

smoked cod with rocket pesto on fettuccine

PREPARATION TIME 15 MINUTES • COOKING TIME 15 MINUTES

375g fettuccine
500g smoked cod fillets

ROCKET PESTO
150g baby rocket leaves
2 cloves garlic, crushed
1/4 cup (40g) toasted pine nuts
1/4 cup (35g) toasted pistachios
2 tablespoons lemon juice
1/2 cup (40g) coarsely grated parmesan cheese
1 cup (250ml) olive oil

1 Cook pasta in large saucepan of boiling water, uncovered, until
  tender; drain.

2 While pasta is cooking, cook fish in large non-stick frying pan until
  browned both sides; cool 5 minutes then flake with fork into large bowl.

3 Place pasta in large bowl with fish and rocket pesto; toss gently
  to combine.

rocket pesto Blend or process all ingredients to form a paste.

SERVES 4

per serving 74.2g fat; 4598kJ

tip Pesto can be made up to 2 days ahead and kept, covered, in the
refrigerator. Pesto can also be frozen for up to 3 months.

smoked salmon
lasagne stacks

PREPARATION TIME 15 MINUTES • COOKING TIME 10 MINUTES

8 sheets curly lasagne (approximately 250g)
400g thinly sliced smoked salmon
1 medium avocado (250g), sliced thinly
1/3 cup (80ml) lime juice
1/2 cup (125ml) peanut oil
1 tablespoon finely chopped fresh dill tips
2 teaspoons seeded mustard
100g baby spinach leaves

1 Cook pasta in large saucepan of boiling water, uncovered, until just tender; drain. Rinse under cold water; drain, then pat completely dry with absorbent paper.

2 Place two sheets of pasta on board; layer half of the salmon evenly onto sheets. Top each layer of salmon with another sheet of pasta, avocado, another sheet of pasta and the remaining salmon. Top each of the stacks with a sheet of pasta. Cut each stack in half; halve each piece diagonally. Place two pieces of the stacks on serving plates.

3 Combine juice, oil, dill and mustard in small jug; whisk until dressing is blended. Pour half of the dressing over spinach in medium bowl; toss gently to combine. Drizzle stacks with remaining dressing; serve with spinach.

SERVES 4

per serving 39.1g fat; 2282kJ

linguine with crab

PREPARATION TIME 10 MINUTES • COOKING TIME 15 MINUTES

300g fresh crab meat
1 clove garlic, crushed
2 red thai chillies, seeded,
**   sliced thinly**
1/2 cup (125ml) dry white wine
1 tablespoon finely grated
**   lemon rind**
375g linguine
1/2 cup loosely packed, coarsely
**   chopped fresh flat-leaf parsley**
1 small red onion (100g),
**   sliced thinly**
1/3 cup (80ml) peanut oil

1 Cook crab, garlic and chilli in large heated non-stick frying pan, stirring, until crab is just cooked.

2 Add wine and rind; bring to a boil. Reduce heat; simmer, uncovered, until wine reduces by half.

3 Meanwhile, cook pasta in large saucepan of boiling water, uncovered, until just tender; drain.

4 Place pasta in large bowl with crab mixture and remaining ingredients; toss gently to combine.

SERVES 4

per serving 19.7g fat; 2299kJ

saganaki prawn pasta

PREPARATION TIME 10 MINUTES • COOKING TIME 15 MINUTES

500g medium uncooked prawns
2 teaspoons olive oil
1 small brown onion (100g),
  chopped finely
2 cloves garlic, crushed
600ml bottled tomato pasta sauce
1 cup (250ml) vegetable stock
375g small spirals
200g fetta cheese, crumbled
2 tablespoons coarsely chopped
  fresh oregano

1 Shell and devein prawns, leaving tails intact.

2 Heat oil in medium saucepan; cook onion and garlic, stirring, until onion softens. Add prawns; cook, stirring, until prawns change colour.

3 Add sauce and stock; bring to a boil. Reduce heat; simmer, uncovered, about 2 minutes or until hot.

4 Meanwhile, cook pasta in large saucepan of boiling water, uncovered, until just tender; drain.

5 Place pasta in large bowl with prawn mixture, cheese and oregano; toss gently to combine.

SERVES 4

per serving 15.8g fat; 2495kJ

angel hair seafood laksa

PREPARATION TIME 10 MINUTES • COOKING TIME 15 MINUTES

We used ling fillets in this recipe but you can use any firm white fish fillet you like –
or you can increase the amount of prawns called for and not use any fish.

500g medium uncooked prawns
1 tablespoon laksa paste
2 cups (500ml) vegetable stock
2 cups (500ml) water
400ml coconut cream
300g firm white fish fillets, chopped coarsely
250g angel hair pasta
300g baby bok choy, chopped coarsely
4 green onions, sliced thinly
1/4 cup loosely packed coriander leaves

1 Shell and devein prawns, leaving tails intact.

2 Cook laksa paste in heated large saucepan, stirring, until fragrant.
Stir in prawns, stock, the water, coconut cream and fish; bring to
a boil. Reduce heat; simmer, uncovered, until prawns change colour
and fish is just cooked.

3 Meanwhile, cook pasta in large saucepan of boiling water, uncovered,
until just tender; drain.

4 While pasta is cooking, stir bok choy, onion and coriander into laksa
mixture; cook, uncovered, until bok choy is just wilted.

5 Divide pasta among serving bowls; top with laksa mixture.

SERVES 4

per serving 23.9g fat; 2375kJ
tip Do not make this recipe until just before you want to serve it.

bow ties and salmon
in lemon cream

PREPARATION TIME 10 MINUTES • COOKING TIME 15 MINUTES

375g bow ties
1 medium lemon (140g)
415g can red salmon,
 drained, flaked
¹/₂ cup (125ml) cream
4 green onions, sliced thinly

1 Cook pasta in large saucepan of boiling water, uncovered, until just tender; drain.

2 Meanwhile, using zester, remove rind from lemon. Place rind and pasta in large saucepan with remaining ingredients; stir over low heat until hot.

SERVES 4

per serving 24.7g fat; 2524kJ

tuna with shells, capers, olives and green beans

PREPARATION TIME 15 MINUTES • COOKING TIME 15 MINUTES

375g small shells
200g green beans, halved
3 x 125g cans tuna slices in spring water, drained
150g seeded black olives, halved
1 medium red capsicum (200g), sliced thinly
1/4 cup (60ml) olive oil
1/4 cup (60ml) white wine vinegar
2 tablespoons drained capers, chopped coarsely
1 clove garlic, crushed

1 Cook pasta in large saucepan of boiling water, uncovered, until just tender; drain. Rinse under cold water; drain.

2 Meanwhile, boil, steam or microwave beans until just tender; rinse under cold water, drain.

3 Place pasta and beans in large bowl with tuna, olives, capsicum and combined remaining ingredients; toss gently to combine.

SERVES 4

per serving 16.1g fat; 2505kJ

prawn phad thai

PREPARATION TIME 15 MINUTES • COOKING TIME 10 MINUTES

600g medium uncooked prawns
1 teaspoon grated fresh ginger
2 cloves garlic, crushed
1 red thai chilli, sliced thinly
1¹/₂ tablespoons finely chopped
  palm sugar
¹/₄ cup (60ml) soy sauce
2 tablespoons sweet chilli sauce
1 tablespoon fish sauce
1¹/₂ tablespoons tomato paste
250g angel hair pasta
1 tablespoon sesame oil
6 green onions, sliced thinly
2 cups (160g) bean sprouts
¹/₂ cup loosely packed fresh
  coriander leaves

1 Shell and devein prawns, leaving tails intact. Place prawns in large bowl with ginger, garlic and chilli; toss to combine. Combine sugar, sauces and paste in screw-top jar; shake well.

2 Cook pasta in large saucepan of boiling water, uncovered, until just tender; drain.

3 Meanwhile, heat oil in wok or large frying pan; stir-fry prawn mixture, in batches, until prawns just change in colour. Return prawns to wok, add sauce mixture; stir-fry about 1 minute or until sugar melts. Remove from heat; add onion, sprouts, coriander and pasta, toss gently to combine.

SERVES 4

per serving 6.2g fat; 1590kJ

glossary

almonds
BLANCHED skins removed.
FLAKED paper-thin slices.
SLIVERED small lengthways-cut pieces.

bacon rashers also known as slices of bacon; made from pork side, cured and smoked.

basil
PURPLE also known as royal or opal basil; has an almost clove-like scent.

SWEET has a strong, slightly anise-like smell and is an essential ingredient in many Italian dishes.

THAI also known as bai krapow or holy basil; small, crinkly leaves with a strong, somewhat bitter, flavour. Most often used in Thai food and other Asian dishes.

beans
BORLOTTI also known as Roman beans; pale pink with darker red spots, eaten fresh or dried.

CANNELLINI small, dried white beans similar in appearance and flavour to other *Phaseolus vulgaris*: great northern, navy and haricot beans.

KIDNEY medium-sized red beans, slightly floury yet sweet in flavour; sold dried or canned, used in soups, stews, etc.

YELLOW STRING also known as wax, French, butter and runner; basically yellow-coloured fresh "green" beans.

beetroot also known as red beets or, simply, beets.

breadcrumbs
PACKAGED fine-textured, crunchy, purchased, white breadcrumbs.

STALE one- or two-day-old bread made into crumbs by grating by hand, blending or processing.

butter use salted or unsalted ("sweet") butter; 125g is equal to one stick of butter.

buttermilk sold alongside fresh milk products in supermarkets; low-fat milk cultured to give a slightly sour, tangy taste. Low-fat yogurt can be substituted.

capers the grey-green buds of a warm climate (usually Mediterranean) shrub sold either dried and salted or pickled in a vinegar brine; used in sauces and dressings.

cheese
HALOUMI firm, cream-coloured sheep milk cheese matured in brine; somewhat like a minty, salty fetta, haloumi can be grilled or fried, briefly, without breaking down.

GOAT made from goat milk, has an earthy, strong taste; available in both soft and firm textures.

PIZZA a commercial blend of varying proportions of processed grated cheddar, mozzarella and parmesan.

chickpeas also called garbanzos, hummus or channa; an irregularly round, sandy-coloured legume widely used in Mediterranean cooking.

chillies available in many types and sizes, both fresh and dried. Wear rubber gloves to seed and chop fresh chillies as they can burn your skin. Removing membranes and seeds lessens the heat level.

coriander also known as cilantro or Chinese parsley; has bright green leaves and a pungent flavour. The entire plant – roots, stems and leaves – is often called for in recipes from Southeast Asia and Mexico.

cos lettuce also known as romaine lettuce; legend has it that this long-leafed salad green originated on the island of Cos in the Aegean Sea. This is the traditional Caesar salad lettuce.

cream
FRESH (MINIMUM FAT CONTENT 35%) also known as pure cream and pouring cream; contains no additives.

LIGHT SOUR (MINIMUM FAT CONTENT 18%) cream specifically cultured to produce its characteristic tart flavour; thinner than normal sour cream so should not be substituted in cooking because the consistency will affect recipe results.

lebanese cucumber

SOUR (MINIMUM FAT CONTENT 35%) a thick, commercially cultured soured cream. Good with baked potatoes and for dips, toppings and baked cheesecakes.

CRÈME FRAÎCHE (MINIMUM FAT CONTENT 35%) velvety texture and tangy taste; available in cartons from delicatessens and supermarkets.

cucumber, lebanese short, slender and thin-skinned; also known as European or burpless cucumbers.

dill pickles also known as kosher dills; small cucumbers that have been pickled in a brine of white vinegar, dill, clove and other spices.

eggplant also known as aubergine.

eggs some recipes call for raw or barely cooked eggs; exercise caution if there is a salmonella problem in your area.

endive a curly-leafed green vegetable, most often used in salads.

fennel a fresh green bulb also known as finocchio or anise; eaten raw in salads and braised or fried as a vegetable accompaniment. Also the name given to the dried seeds which have a licorice flavour.

fish fillets fish pieces that have been boned and skinned.

gherkins the word used to described both the small young cucumbers grown especially for pickling and the already pickled and bottled finished product; these are sometimes known as cornichons.

ginger
FRESH also known as green or root ginger; the thick gnarled root of a tropical plant.

GROUND also known as powdered ginger; used as a flavouring in cakes, pies and puddings but cannot be substituted for fresh ginger.

green peppercorns soft, unripe berry of the pepper plant usually sold packed in brine (occasionally found dried, packed in salt).

herbs when specified, we used dried (not ground) herbs in the proportion of 1:4 for fresh herbs; eg 1 teaspoon dried herbs equals 4 teaspoons (1 tablespoon) chopped fresh herbs.

kumara Polynesian name of orange-fleshed sweet potato often confused with yam.

lemon grass a tall, clumping, lemon-smelling and tasting, sharp-edged grass; the white lower part of each stem is chopped and used in Asian cooking or for tea.

marsala a sweet fortified wine originally from Sicily.

teardrop tomatoes

mesclun a mixture of baby lettuces and other salad leaves, also known as gourmet salad mix; sometimes contains the petals of various flowers.

mince meat also known as ground meat.

mint a tangy, aromatic green herb available fresh or dried; of the 30 or so varieties, pungent peppermint and the milder spearmint are most commonly used in cooking.

mushrooms

BUTTON small, cultivated white mushrooms with a delicate, subtle flavour.

DRIED PORCINI also known as dried cèpes; a rich-flavoured wild mushroom which is reconstituted and used often in Italian cooking.

SWISS BROWN light to dark brown mushrooms with full-bodied flavour. Also known as portobello. Button mushrooms can be substituted.

onions

GREEN also known as scallions or (incorrectly) shallots; immature onions picked before the bulbs have formed, having long, bright-green edible stalks.

RED also known as Spanish, or Bermuda onions; sweet-flavoured, large, purple-red onions that are particularly good eaten raw.

SPRING have crisp, narrow, green-leafed tops and large sweet white bulbs; best eaten raw in salads.

palm sugar also known as jaggery or gula jawa; a moulded lump sugar made from distilled palm juice. Available from Asian specialty shops; dark brown sugar can be substituted if necessary.

pesto an Italian paste or thick uncooked sauce, traditionally made with fresh basil, garlic, parmesan cheese, olive oil and pine nuts, and served with pasta or soups. Bottled versions, made from such ingredients as sun-dried tomatoes, roasted vegetables and coriander are available from most supermarkets and delicatessens.

polenta a flour-like cereal made of ground corn (maize); similar to cornmeal but finer and lighter in colour. Also the name of the dish that is made from it.

preserved lemons a North African specialty; lemons are quartered and preserved in salt and lemon juice. Only the rind is used.

prosciutto salt-cured, air-dried (unsmoked), pressed ham; usually sold in paper-thin slices, ready to eat.

red curry paste combination of dried red chillies, onions, garlic, oil, lemon rind, shrimp paste, ground cumin, paprika, ground turmeric and ground black pepper.

rocket also known as arugula, rugula and rucola; peppery-tasting green leaf that should be used similarly to baby spinach – eaten raw in salads or cooked in soups, risottos and frittatas.

saffron stigma of a member of the crocus family, available in strands or ground form; imparts a yellow-orange colour to food once infused in hot water. Very expensive, it should be stored in freezer.

seafood marinara mix a mixture of uncooked chopped seafood available from fishmarkets and fishmongers.

sesame oil made from roasted, crushed white sesame seeds. Do not use for frying.

snow peas also called mange tout (eat all). Snow pea tendrils are the growing shoots of the plant.

tamarind concentrate a thick, purple-black, ready-to-use paste extracted from the pulp of the tamarind bean; it is used as is, with no soaking, stirred into sauces and casseroles.

tomatoes

BOTTLED PASTA SAUCE we used an Italian-made all-natural sauce of chopped tomato, tomato paste, onion, salt and sugar sold in 600ml glass jars.

CHERRY tiny, marble-shaped tomatoes. Use raw (whole or halved) in salads or cooked in various pasta dishes. Also used as decoration or garnish.

PASTE triple-concentrated tomato puree used to add flavour to soups, casseroles and sauces.

SEMI-DRIED partially dried tomato sections, usually sold marinated in herbed olive oil. They are soft enough to be consumed without needing to be reconstituted.

SUN-DRIED totally dehydrated tomatoes sold bottled in oil or packaged in plastic; they need to be reconstituted before being eaten. We used sun-dried tomatoes in oil, unless otherwise specified.

TEARDROP also known as pear tomatoes; small teardrop-shaped yellow or red tomatoes that are used in the same way as cherry tomatoes.

turmeric a member of the ginger family, its roots are dried and ground, resulting in the rich yellow powder that gives many Indian dishes their characteristic colour.

vanilla bean dried long, thin pod from a tropical golden orchid; its tiny black seeds impart vanilla flavour when used in cooking.

vietnamese mint not a mint at all, this narrow-leafed, pungent herb, also known as Cambodian mint, daun laksa and laksa leaf, is widely used in Southeast Asian soups and salads.

vine leaves grapevine leaves sold packaged in brine, either bottled or in cryovac packets.

vinegar

BALSAMIC authentic only from the province of Modena, Italy; made from a regional wine of white Trebbiano grapes specially processed then aged in antique wooden casks to give the exquisite pungent flavour.

RASPBERRY white wine vinegar in which fresh raspberries have been steeped, imparting their flavour.

RICE WINE also known as seasoned rice vinegar; made from fermented rice and flavoured with sugar and salt.

WHITE made from spirit of cane sugar.

wonton wrappers gow gee, egg or spring roll pastry sheets can be substituted to enclose various meat or vegetable fillings. Wonton wrappers provide a simple solution to making ravioli and tortellini at home.

worcestershire sauce a thin, dark-brown spicy sauce that is used both as a seasoning and condiment.

zucchini also known as courgette, belonging to the squash family. The yellow flowers, sometimes with baby vegetables still attached, are available in specialist greengrocers. Stuffed with savoury fillings then deep-fried, they are often part of an antipasti platter.

index

make your own stock

These recipes can be made up to 4 days ahead and stored, covered, in the refrigerator. Be sure to remove any fat from the surface after the cooled stock has been refrigerated overnight. If the stock is to be kept longer, it is best to freeze it in smaller quantities.
All stock recipes make about 2.5 litres (10 cups).

Stock is also available in cans or tetra packs. Stock cubes or powder can be used. As a guide, 1 teaspoon of stock powder or 1 small crumbled stock cube mixed with 1 cup (250ml) water will give a fairly strong stock. Be aware of the salt and fat content of stock cubes and powders and prepared stocks.

BEEF STOCK

2kg meaty beef bones
2 medium onions (300g)
2 sticks celery, chopped
2 medium carrots (250g), chopped
3 bay leaves
2 teaspoons black peppercorns
5 litres (20 cups) water
3 litres (12 cups) water, extra

Place bones and unpeeled chopped onions in baking dish. Bake in hot oven about 1 hour or until bones and onions are well browned. Transfer bones and onions to large pan, add celery, carrots, bay leaves, peppercorns and water, simmer, uncovered, 3 hours. Add extra water, simmer, uncovered, further 1 hour; strain.

CHICKEN STOCK

2kg chicken bones
2 medium onions (300g), chopped
2 sticks celery, chopped
2 medium carrots (250g), chopped
3 bay leaves
2 teaspoons black peppercorns
5 litres (20 cups) water

Combine all ingredients in large pan, simmer, uncovered, 2 hours; strain.

VEGETABLE STOCK

2 large carrots (360g), chopped
2 large parsnips (360g), chopped
4 medium onions (600g), chopped
12 sticks celery, chopped
4 bay leaves
2 teaspoons black peppercorns
6 litres (24 cups) water

Combine all ingredients in large pan, simmer, uncovered, 1½ hours; strain.

conversion chart

measures

One Australian metric measuring cup holds approximately 250ml, one Australian metric tablespoon holds 20ml, one Australian metric teaspoon holds 5ml.

The difference between one country's measuring cups and another's is within a two- or three-teaspoon variance, and will not affect your cooking results. North America, New Zealand and the United Kingdom use a 15ml tablespoon.

All cup and spoon measurements are level. The most accurate way of measuring dry ingredients is to weigh them. When measuring liquids, use a clear glass or plastic jug with the metric markings.

We use large eggs with an average weight of 60g.

dry measures

METRIC	IMPERIAL
15g	½oz
30g	1oz
60g	2oz
90g	3oz
125g	4oz (¼lb)
155g	5oz
185g	6oz
220g	7oz
250g	8oz (½lb)
280g	9oz
315g	10oz
345g	11oz
375g	12oz (¾lb)
410g	13oz
440g	14oz
470g	15oz
500g	16oz (1lb)
750g	24oz (1½lb)
1kg	32oz (2lb)

liquid measures

METRIC	IMPERIAL
30ml	1 fluid oz
60ml	2 fluid oz
100ml	3 fluid oz
125ml	4 fluid oz
150ml	5 fluid oz (¼ pint/1 gill)
190ml	6 fluid oz
250ml	8 fluid oz
300ml	10 fluid oz (½ pint)
500ml	16 fluid oz
600ml	20 fluid oz (1 pint)
1000ml (1 litre)	1¾ pints

length measures

METRIC	IMPERIAL
3mm	⅛in
6mm	¼in
1cm	½in
2cm	¾in
2.5cm	1in
5cm	2in
6cm	2½in
8cm	3in
10cm	4in
13cm	5in
15cm	6in
18cm	7in
20cm	8in
23cm	9in
25cm	10in
28cm	11in
30cm	12in (1ft)

oven temperatures

These oven temperatures are only a guide for conventional ovens.
For fan-forced ovens, check the manufacturer's manual.

	°C (CELSIUS)	°F (FAHRENHEIT)	GAS MARK
Very slow	120	250	½
Slow	150	275-300	1-2
Moderately slow	160	325	3
Moderate	180	350-375	4-5
Moderately hot	200	400	6
Hot	220	425-450	7-8
Very hot	240	475	9

ARE YOU MISSING SOME OF THE WORLD'S FAVOURITE COOKBOOKS?

The Australian Women's Weekly Cookbooks are available from bookshops, cookshops, supermarkets and other stores all over the world. You can also buy direct from the publisher, using the order form below.

TITLE	RRP	QTY	TITLE	RRP	QTY
Asian Meals in Minutes	£6.99		Great Lamb Cookbook	£6.99	
Babies & Toddlers Good Food	£6.99		Greek Cooking Class	£6.99	
Barbecue Meals In Minutes	£6.99		Healthy Heart Cookbook	£6.99	
Basic Cooking Class	£6.99		Indian Cooking Class	£6.99	
Beginners Cooking Class	£6.99		Japanese Cooking Class	£6.99	
Beginners Simple Meals	£6.99		Kids' Birthday Cakes	£6.99	
Beginners Thai	£6.99		Kids Cooking	£6.99	
Best Food	£6.99		Lean Food	£6.99	
Best Food Desserts	£6.99		Low-carb, Low-fat	£6.99	
Best Food Fast	£6.99		Low-fat Feasts	£6.99	
Best Food Mains	£6.99		Low-fat Food For Life	£6.99	
Cakes, Biscuits & Slices	£6.99		Low-fat Meals in Minutes	£6.99	
Cakes Cooking Class	£6.99		Main Course Salads	£6.99	
Caribbean Cooking	£6.99		Middle Eastern Cooking Class	£6.99	
Casseroles	£6.99		Midweek Meals in Minutes	£6.99	
Chicken	£6.99		Muffins, Scones & Breads	£6.99	
Chicken Meals in Minutes	£6.99		New Casseroles	£6.99	
Chinese Cooking Class	£6.99		New Classics	£6.99	
Christmas Cooking	£6.99		New Finger Food	£6.99	
Chocolate	£6.99		Party Food and Drink	£6.99	
Cocktails	£6.99		Pasta Meals in Minutes	£6.99	
Cooking for Friends	£6.99		Potatoes	£6.99	
Creative Cooking on a Budget	£6.99		Salads: Simple, Fast & Fresh	£6.99	
Detox	£6.99		Saucery	£6.99	
Dinner Beef	£6.99		Sauces, Salsas & Dressings	£6.99	
Dinner Lamb	£6.99		Sensational Stir-Fries	£6.99	
Dinner Seafood	£6.99		Short-order Cook	£6.99	
Easy Australian Style	£6.99		Slim	£6.99	
Easy Curry	£6.99		Sweet Old-fashioned Favourites	£6.99	
Easy Spanish-style Cookery	£6.99		Thai Cooking Class	£6.99	
Essential Soup	£6.99		Vegetarian Meals in Minutes	£6.99	
Freezer, Meals from the	£6.99		Vegie Food	£6.99	
French Food, New	£6.99		Weekend Cook	£6.99	
Fresh Food for Babies & Toddlers	£6.99		Wicked Sweet Indulgences	£6.99	
Get Real, Make a Meal	£6.99		Wok Meals in Minutes	£6.99	
Good Food Fast	£6.99		TOTAL COST:	£	

Mr/Mrs/Ms _____

Address _____

_____ Postcode _____

Day time phone _____ Email* (optional) _____

I enclose my cheque/money order for £ _____

or please charge £ _____

to my: ☐ Access ☐ Mastercard ☐ Visa ☐ Diners Club

PLEASE NOTE: WE DO NOT ACCEPT SWITCH OR ELECTRON CARDS

Card number [ ][ ][ ][ ] [ ][ ][ ][ ] [ ][ ][ ][ ] [ ][ ][ ][ ]

Expiry date _____ 3 digit security code (found on reverse of card) _____

Cardholder's name_____ Signature _____

To order: Mail or fax – photocopy or complete the order form above, and send your credit card details or cheque payable to: Australian Consolidated Press (UK), Moulton Park Business Centre, Red House Road, Moulton Park, Northampton NN3 6AQ, phone (+44) (0) 1604 497531 fax (+44) (0) 1604 497533, e-mail books@acpmedia.co.uk or order online at www.acpuk.com

Non-UK residents: We accept the credit cards listed on the coupon, or cheques, drafts or International Money Orders payable in sterling and drawn on a UK bank. Credit card charges are at the exchange rate current at the time of payment.

Postage and packing UK: Add £1.00 per order plus 50p per book.

Postage and packing overseas: Add £2.00 per order plus £1.00 per book.

All pricing current at time of going to press and subject to change/availability.

Offer ends 31.12.2007

* By including your email address, you consent to receipt of any email regarding this magazine, and other emails which inform you of ACP's other publications, products, services and events, and to promote third party goods and services you may be interested in.